God and the Soul

STUDIES IN ETHICS AND THE
PHILOSOPHY OF RELIGION

The Series is meant to provide an opportunity for philosophical discussions of a limited length which pursue in some detail specific topics in ethics or the philosophy of religion, or topics which belong to both fields. For the most part, the Series will present work by contemporary philosophers. The contributors, while not representing any single philosophical school, will be in sympathy with recent developments in philosophy. Occasionally, however, unpublished material by earlier philosophers, or works of importance which are now out of print, or not easily accessible, will appear in the Series.

D. Z. PHILLIPS

God and the Soul

by

PETER GEACH

London
ROUTLEDGE & KEGAN PAUL

First published in 1969
by Routledge & Kegan Paul Limited
Broadway House, 68-74 Carter Lane
London, E.C.4
Printed in Great Britain by
The Garden City Press Limited
Letchworth, Hertfordshire
© *Peter Geach* 1969
SBN 7100 6323 7

Contents

	ANALYTICAL TABLE OF CONTENTS	*page* vii
	PREFACE	xxi
1.	REINCARNATION	1
2.	IMMORTALITY	17
3.	WHAT DO WE THINK WITH?	30
4.	FORM AND EXISTENCE	42
5.	WHAT ACTUALLY EXISTS	65
6.	CAUSALITY AND CREATION	75
7.	PRAYING FOR THINGS TO HAPPEN	86
8.	ON WORSHIPPING THE RIGHT GOD	100
9.	THE MORAL LAW AND THE LAW OF GOD	117
	INDEX	131

Analytical Table of Contents

1. *Reincarnation*

Reincarnation as here discussed consists in one and the same human mind's successively animating two different *human* bodies. I shall not consider supposed cases where a mind animates now a human, now a non-human body; and I confine myself to Western conceptions   pp. 1–2

Given some human body or other, there is the same person just so long as there is the same mind   pp. 2–3

Locke's doctrine of personal identity is indefensible; and his view of responsibility is morally repugnant pp. 3–4

Do we understand propositions like 'I lived in pre-Christian Rome' apart from memory? This could be maintained if we accepted such views of the meaning of 'I' as McTaggart and Descartes argued for. But we must remember that there can be a spurious impression of having understood an incoherent supposition   pp. 4–5

The arguments of McTaggart and Descartes were designed to show that each one of us can arrive at indubitable empirical propositions about the individual that he signifies by 'I', in a certain soliloquistic use of this word   pp. 6–7

These propositions are to be *indubitable* answers to questions like 'Who is now in pain?'. 'Who is now puzzled?' But since the ordinary answers to these 'Who' questions are by stipulation excluded, the questions have been deprived of sense   p. 7

Descartes fell into the Masked Man fallacy   p. 8

In many soliloquistic uses, 'I' does not refer to an individual. Though 'I' in soliloquy *can* refer to the person speaking, such cases are no help to Descartes   pp. 8–9

Could 'I' refer, not to some personality, in the 'multiple personality' sense? The criterion of identity for personalities is obscure; and we are hardly likely to make intelligible the transference of a personality from one body to another   pp. 9–10

But suppose a man's 'memories' of his life as Julius Caesar were borne out by historical facts they led us to discover?   pp. 10–11

We need to grasp certain truths about memory:

(1) There are false memories   p. 11

(2) There is no inner self-authenticating sign by which to tell memory-knowledge from possibly false memory-belief; this does not justify scepticism   pp. 11–12

(3) There are episodic memory-judgments   pp. 12–13

(4) A judgment does not count as a memory-judgment if it has an unacceptable provenance, e.g. other people's information or post-hypnotic suggestion   pp. 13–14

If a surgeon could stuff someone else's brain with 'memories' of my life, these would not be memories; nor would a person thus claiming to be Peter Geach actually be Peter Geach   pp. 14–15

'Memories' of what Julius Caesar did would raise an irremovable doubt as to whether their claim to be memories is not vitiated by their provenance   p. 15

The argument about what 'only Julius Caesar can have known' is grossly inconsistent if applied to such 'memories'   p. 15

So the notion of reincarnation we have been examining has no clear sense   p. 16

2. *Immortality*

I shall be discussing survival of bodily death, rather than endless survival   p. 17

There is no evidence for survival of a 'subtle body'

pp. 17–18

The Platonic view ascribes all experience to the mind or soul; this opens up the logical possibility of a mind's persisting with similar experiences when the body perishes

pp. 18–19

But words like 'pain' or 'seeing' do not get their meaning either from the very experience so named, or from a private uncheckable performance of conferring their meaning. And we do not know how to apply such concepts to immaterial spirits   pp. 19–20

A concept like *seeing* or *feeling* collapses if we break its threads of connexion with other concepts relating to the physical properties of perceived bodies and to human bodily behaviour   pp. 12–22

A disembodied spirit without sensuous experiences would not be a surviving human person; 'my soul is not I'

p. 22

And even though a spirit might persist as a remnant of a person, its very individuality would depend on a permanent *capacity* for such reunion with a body as would reconstitute the dead human being   pp. 22–24

Could this capacity be realized by reincarnation? It is hard to give a clear sense to this   pp. 24–25

Nor could the mental phenomena of mediumship be evidence of survival   pp. 25–26

In this life a one-one relation of material continuity of body is a necessary condition of personal identity, though no actual bit of matter need persist in the body. A similar one-one relation between the old body and the new would be needed in order that we might justifiably speak of the same human being's living again   pp. 26–27

Continuity of memory would not be sufficient pp. 27–28

So there is no reasonable hope of surviving death unless we hold the Jewish and Christian hope of the resurrection of the body   pp. 28–29

3. *What do we think with?*

Materialists hold that we think with the brain; immaterialists, that we think with an immaterial part, the mind or soul. Both may be wrong   p. 30

'Thinking', unlike 'meaning' and 'understanding', is a word for an activity   pp. 31–32

Some activities are more basic than others; doing a less basic action always consists in doing a more basic action, within a certain assumed context   pp. 32–33

A less basic action need not be describable as performed with an instrument N, and may still less be ascribable to N, merely because the corresponding more basic action is so   p. 33

So, if thinking were not basic, it might be wrong to ascribe it to the brain even though an activity that was more basic in relation to thinking were rightly ascribable to the brain. But so far as I can see thinking *is* basic   pp. 33–34

There is no 'stream of thought'; thoughts form a discrete series with no gradual transitions   pp. 34–35

Individual occurrent thoughts occur neither *legato* nor *staccato;* thoughts occupy neither single instants, nor yet (like sensory processes) divisible stretches, of physical time   p. 36

Non-basic actions, e.g. murders, are similarly not clockable (except by arbitrary legal decision); but we ought not to assimilate thought to this sort of action—thought *is* basic   p. 37

Since no physiological process has the same time-relations as a thought, thought cannot be the activity of a bodily part and materialism is false   p. 37

But the immaterialistic idea that man has an immaterial part to think with is incoherent   p. 38

Could thought occur apart from a living organism? Thought is more than contingently related to language; and language could be produced in such circumstances as supplied strong evidence that thoughts were being originated and not originated by any living organism   p. 39

Persistence of such thoughts could constitute the survival of a 'separated soul'   pp. 39–40

Machines manifestly do not think, for they are not even alive   pp. 40–41

4. *Form and existence*

I am discussing what Aquinas meant by his term 'act of existing', or 'that by which so-and-so exists'; so first I discuss 'that by which' and 'exists'   p. 42

I. With a predicate '*F*' other than 'exists', 'that by which *x* is *F*' is in Aquinas's language a variant expression for 'the *F*ness of *x*'. These expressions serve to designate *forms* p. 42

The real distinction between a form and the self-subsistent individual (*suppositum*) whose form it is corresponds, for Aquinas, to the logical distinction between subject and predicate. This view is incompatible with the two-name theory of prediction   pp. 42–43

There is something a predicate *stands for*. It is to what a predicate stands for, and to that alone, that we can significantly ascribe oneness or manyness. This account is true both of Aquinas's forms and of Frege's *Begriffe* pp. 44–45

A common nature is not named by an abstract singular term, and all such terms are removable by paraphrase
                                                           pp. 46–47

Frege was wrong in holding that a phrase like 'the concept *man*' in subject position stands for an object that 'represents' a *Begriff*. An abstract noun or noun-phrase referring to a form cannot be the *whole* of a logical subject; we must also use a phrase like 'of Socrates' to mention the individual whose form it is   pp. 47–48

'The wisdom of Socrates' is not analysable as 'wisdom which Socrates possesses', but splits up into 'the wisdom of . . . ' and 'Socrates'. This is like the way that '$\sqrt{25}$' splits up into a functional sign (for the square root) and a numeral   pp. 48–50

We may clarify Aquinas's terminology if for the designata of phrases like 'the wisdom of Socrates' we use the distinctive term 'individualized forms'   pp. 50–51

Although 'the wisdom of . . . ' and 'the power of . . . ' stand for different forms, 'God' and 'the wisdom of God' and 'the power of God' will all, on Aquinas's view, be designations of the same thing; just as the number 1 is the same number as the square of 1 and as the cube of 1

pp. 51–52

On the other hand, if something is red and square, what makes it red is a different *individualized* form from what makes it square. A wave is a familiar example of an individualized form

pp. 52–53

II. Is 'exists' properly predicable of individuals? The thesis that 'exist' is not a predicate is meant to explain how we can significantly and truly deny existence. But there may be other explanations of this puzzle pp. 53–54

There are in fact three logically different kinds of existential proposition; negative examples are most easily distinguished. (A) A proposition like 'Cerberus does not exist' relates to (and does not *exemplify*) a certain use of a proper name, and serves to deny that in this use the name does name anything pp. 55–56

(B) A proposition like 'dragons do not exist' or 'intra-Mercurian planets do not exist' is logically the negative predication of the general term that is the grammatical subject p. 56

The question whether there is *a* so-and-so (*an est?*) is answered with a B proposition. This answer does not relate to what Aquinas calls *esse*. 'God exists' is a B proposition, because 'God' is a descriptive term and not a proper name

pp. 57–58

(C) 'Joseph is not and Simeon is not' (*Genesis* 42: 36) is a sort of proposition using 'is' or 'exists' as when one speaks of an individual's *still* existing, *coming to* exist, etc. 'Is' or 'exists' is here a genuine predicate. A name does not cease to have reference because its bearer perishes pp. 58–60

Existence in sense C always means the persistence of some form in an individual. This is Aquinas's *esse* p. 60

III. Is an individualized form really distinct from that by which the individualized form *is?* e.g. the redness of

Socrates's nose, from that by which this redness *is?*   p. 60

Aquinas's first argument: things that share *F*ness resemble each other in respect of being *F* but differ in respect of *esse*. The point of this difference in respect of *esse* is that e.g. one *F*ness can *cease to be* independently of another

p. 61

Aquinas's second argument: being more or less intense is not a qualitative change, but is a matter of the degree to which a given individualized form exists   pp. 61–62

Aquinas's third argument: to explain the likeness and the difference between a thought of an *X* and a real *X*, he says that there is in both cases an individualized *X*ness, but the manner of *esse* of *X*ness is different in the thinking mind and the thing thought of   pp. 62–64

His sort of 'hairsplitting' may well be the only way to attain the truth   p. 64

5. What actually exists

Provisionally we may say: X actually exists if and only if X either acts, or undergoes change, or both. Actual existence is quite different from the existence expressed in 'There is a so-and-so'   p. 65

Vernacular expressions like 'any *A*', 'each *A*', 'the same *A*', another *A*', *prima facie* commit their user to recognizing *A*s as a kind of object   p. 66

By asserting existential propositions in arithmetic and geometry, *prima facie* we are recognizing certain kinds of non-actual objects as *existing*. There appear to be no definitely statable difficulties about this   p. 67

No demythologizing of arithmetic and geometry is even plausible   p. 68

But the paradoxes of general set theory are a good reason for scepticism about its ontology (which must be an ontology of non-actual objects); and we ought to be still more sceptical about abstract objects that have no clear criterion of identity   p. 68

Do expressions like 'the squareness of the table' and 'the

cat's being on the mat' designate actual entities? Scholastics would give one criterion for the identity of such individuals; Cambridge philosophers of our time, another criterion; the dispute appears silly p. 69

Again, the phrases that purport to designate such entities are often nominalizations of sentences, and it seems that they can easily be removed by paraphrase pp. 69–70

But some accidental individuals, e.g. surfaces and holes, appear less easily dispensable p. 70

There is no reason to try to explain away people and things in terms of events; and the criteria of identity for events are very obscure. But on the other hand some events, e.g. sounds, appear to be directly identifiable individuals.
pp. 70–71

Moreover, unless we recognize events as actual individuals, we cannot explain the difference we surely have to recognize between 'real' changes and mere 'Cambridge' changes pp. 71–72

Further, mental acts like thoughts are surely actualities
p. 72

Occurrent actualities, e.g. sounds and 'real' changes, would take time to be actual; and so, presumably, do substances, which cannot be actual for less time than they take to perform their characteristic activities pp. 72–73

Conceivably, a being could have thoughts and plans, and initiate changes, without undergoing 'real' changes of any sort p. 73

Such a life would be eternal, not just temporally uniform
pp. 73–74

Those who reject such an idea of God may really wish to worship a *non-actual* God p. 74

6. *Causality and Creation*

Is a deductive causal demonstration of God's existence possible? p. 75

Hume is supposed to have proved it possible. But neither Hume nor his admirers specify the logical form of casual propositions. So this assertion is completely idle pp. 75–76

The sense of 'cause' in a casual proof must be derived from familiar examples of causality, not from a metaphysical vision of dependence   pp. 76–77

Aquinas, I think, meant at least the first three 'ways' to be logical demonstrations. Whether they are will depend on the formal logic of causal propositions   p. 77

The general objections to the utility of deductions are all either trivial or fallacious   pp. 78–79

A syllogistic causal argument for God's existence would indeed be impossible; but a proof involving the logic of relations cannot be ruled out in advance   pp. 79–81

There are at least two important classes of causal propositions. (A) Some often come in the form '—is the cause of—', where the blanks are filled with abstract-noun phrases. This is a misleading form; the form 'p because q', where 'because' joins two clauses, is logically preferable as a paradigm for this class   pp. 81–82

(B) There are propositions saying of some agent that he brought something about; these will obviously be needed in talking about God's activity   pp. 82–83

The logical difference between God's creating an *A* and God's making an already existing thing to be *A* is closely analogous to the difference between a man's 'just' looking for 'a' detective story and his looking for 'a particular' detective story; the difference may be shown in both cases by the shift of a quantifier   pp. 83–85

There is much hard logical work to be done on causal propositions. We need not fear that on these frontiers of theology it is irreverent to apply logic   p. 85

7. *Praying for things to happen*

Whatever some people may think, Christians do pray for things to happen. I am here concerned only with prayers for ordinary observable happenings, not for grace or for miracles   p. 86

Christians believe, moreover, that God gives us some

things not only *as* we wish but *because* we wish. This does
not make prayer magically compulsive   p. 87

But it does imply that what happens *because of* prayer is
not something that would have been given by God anyhow.
Since the prayer might not have been offered, the thing
prayed for might have never come about; but it also could
come about, since it did so; therefore, before it happened
it had two-way contingency   pp. 88–89

What is past at the time of a prayer cannot then have
two-way contingency. So we cannot rationally pray for
something to *have* happened; for in using the imperative
of prayer we represent a situation as still to be brought
about, which is incompatible with representing it as past,
as a *fait accompli*   pp. 89–91

'Time does not exist from God's point of view' is a
muddled way of saying that time is a delusion. But time
cannot consistently be treated as a delusion; and so to treat
it would be ruinous to the Judaeo-Christian doctrine of
creation   pp. 91–93

God is unchangeable; but because of changes in creatures
we have to use different propositions at different times to
say *what* God knows or can do; and God sees the world *as*
changing, because it does change   p. 93

It is rational to pray only concerning future contingent
issues. Are there any such issues? Or are all events already
determined in their causes? The applications of probability
theory go to show that what we should commonly count as
chance events (e.g. the fall of dice) really are contingent
in relation to created causes: though they fall under the
order of the Divine Reason, and this accounts for our
ability to find a pattern even in chance events   pp. 93–95

Contingency in the natural world is necessary in order
that human choices may have scope to affect the natural
world. It is in this realm of contingency that we may hope
for prayers to be granted   pp. 95–97

Can we say that after a prayer God brings about what he
was not going to bring about before the prayer? It is not

xvi

• •

clear that saying so would involve a 'real' change in God's will   pp. 97 99

But the notion of 'real' change, even as applied to creatures, is obscure   p. 99

8. *On worshipping the right God*

The view that all *bona fide* worshippers worship the same God is emphatically contradicted by Scripture and Christian tradition   pp. 100–101

What is divine worship, *latria?* Honour that is paid to a symbol recognized as such is not divine worship. The difference between *latria* and lesser worship (*dulia*) is in part conventional (it is a matter of what acts are taken to mean); but sacrifice, and prayers for pardon and grace and glory, are of their nature acts of *latria*   pp. 101–102

Praying to the saints, whether justifiable or not, is not *latria*   p. 102

By 'idolatry' I mean divine worship paid to a human artefact. This may be like a child's half-belief in the personality of her dolls. But there may be explicit belief that a God is specially present *in* the image. Though some people imagine that this belief is never actually held, it has in fact been common in high cultures   pp. 103–104

Astral worship is a similar misbelief   p. 104

We cannot feel complacently superior: idolatry may creep into worship of the true God, and the consultation of 'thinking' machines as oracles might become an idolatry
pp. 104–105

Idolatry is *folly*, even for natural reason if uncorrupted by tradition. It is not arguable that in these matters natural reason is incompetent; and natural reason can discern, and historically has discerned, that the Source of cosmic motion is itself unlike all the moving bodies of the cosmos
pp. 105–106

God *is* specially present in some creatures; but those in which God is specially present are creatures that know and love him, not inanimate bodies like idols or planets p. 106

The Incarnation doctrine is not open to the same objections as idolatry. The dead body of Christ remained united to the Godhead, but this is quite a different case from an idol. Nor is the Eucharist idolatrous   pp. 107–108

If a worshipper does not vainly worship the inanimate, must he be worshipping the only true God? No, for 'to worship' is an intentional verb, and one may worship, as one may admire or love, the non-existent   p. 108

'God' is a descriptive term, not a proper name

pp. 108–109

A senile voter may support a Premier whose very identity is a mere senile confusion; he is not then supporting the real Premier   pp. 109–110

But on the other hand one may succeed in referring to a person although one's description is a bit wrong, and similarly succeed in worshipping the true God in spite of misconceiving his attributes   p. 110

However, a thought that contains a *sufficiently* deviant set of attributes will simply not relate to a given individual at all   pp. 110–111

There may then be worshippers whose thoughts nowise relate to the true God. Such ignorance, even if itself inculpable, may prevent them from turning to God for grace and mercy   pp. 111

There is no reason to think that love on man's side can prevail over any amount of intellectual error, or that God's calling and drawing of man is revealed in all sincere worship

pp. 111–112

There is no safe, tolerable, level of error about God's attributes   pp. 112–113

Natural theology does not deal only with an abstract sort of God, and may lead men to worship the true God. But a natural theologian may err so widely that he does not lay hold of the true God with his heart and mind   pp. 113–114

'A God exists' ascribes, not existence to a God, but Divine attributes to something-or-other; and someone who truly judges that a God exists may be ascribing Divine attributes to an inferior or merely phantom object

pp. 114–115

That we must not be tolerant of errors about the Divinity does not mean that persecution is defensible, but that no labour should be counted too great to win men from the Kingdom of Darkness   pp. 115–116

9. *The moral law and the law of God*

Moral philosophers have long used an argument to show that God's commandments cannot generate moral obligation
p. 117
This argument goes back to Plato's *Euthyphro*
pp. 118–119
Knowledge of God and his commandments is not a prerequisite of *all* moral knowledge; in particular, our knowledge that lying is bad is independent of any revelation
pp. 119–120
But we must know God's law to know that we must not do evil that good may come   p. 120
'Doing evil' here means 'doing what is of itself a bad thing to do', not 'causing somebody or something to suffer evil'   pp. 120–121
Adultery is absolutely out of consideration for someone who accepts that we must not do evil that good may come, but only *prima facie* objectionable for someone who rejects this principle. It is psychologically possible to hold the principle without knowledge of God's law   p. 121
The only logically relevant reply to 'Why shouldn't I?' is an appeal to something that the questioner wants and cannot get if he does the questionable action. The 'You *mustn't*' appeal to a so-called Sense of Duty, regardless of the content of the alleged duty, is irrational and immoral
pp. 121–122
But, as Mrs. Foot has argued, we need, and cannot rationally choose to do without, habits of virtue that would exclude deliberation whether e.g. to commit adultery
pp. 122–123
Still, might one not sacrifice one's integrity of virtue for

the good of others? This is where the law of God becomes
relevant   p. 123

Man's reason can discern that some practices are *generally undersirable*. Unless this realization is in fact a promulgation to man of a Divine law *absolutely forbidding* such practices, most men are left by God with no guidance; for men's wits certainly are not adequate to judge in their own cause and make the right exceptions, and particular Divine guidance is certainly not available to most men   p. 124

A man who can see the general undesirability of such practices has in fact had God's law promulgated to him, and can come to realize this explicitly   pp. 124–125

This is the argument of Hobbes and Berkeley, from 'theorems' about reasonable conduct to knowledge of God's laws properly so called   p. 126

'Why should I obey God's law?' is an insane question; by defiance of an Almighty God 'men may shake off their ease, but not their yoke'   pp. 126–127

Worship of the Supreme Power casts out all fear of tyrants' threats. It is reasonable that knowledge of our situation—knowledge that we are absolutely in God's power —should affect our moral code   pp. 127–128

God's Providence can assure that no man is inculpably faced with a choice of violating one or other of God's prohibitions   p. 128

This fear of God is only the beginning of wisdom; but without it there is only folly   pp. 128–129

Sinners cannot count on being able for ever to misuse God's creatures in defiance of his commandments   p. 129

Preface

The papers on 'Reincarnation' and 'Immortality' were written before my book *Mental Acts* and later revised; in that book I borrowed material from both papers, particularly from the second one, freely adapting it to the purposes of the book. The papers on 'Form and Existence' and 'What Actually Exists' appeared originally in *Proceedings of The Aristotelian Society*, Vol. LV and Supp. Vol. XLII respectively, and are reprinted by permission of the Editor of the Aristotelian Society. (Copyright: The Aristotelian Society, 1954–55 and 1968, respectively.) 'Form and Existence' appears here with some stylistic changes, and with a brief paragraph added on p. 58, to remove an objection that occurred to some readers. I still think this paper gives a correct account of Aquinas' views; 'What Actually Exists' states some difficulties that have occurred to me since 1954, about accepting these views as true. 'Causality and Creation' was published in *Sophia*, Vol. I, No. 1, 1962, and also in *Ensign*, Spring No., Dublin, 1967. 'The Moral Law and The Law of God' was published in a much simplified form in *Cardinal*, an undergraduate periodical at Birmingham. The other papers have not been published previously.

PETER GEACH

Leeds, 1968

1

Reincarnation

The supposed occurrence for which I shall here use the term 'reincarnation' consists in one and the same human mind's successively animating two different human bodies. I use the verb 'animate' for the relation of a man X's mind to X's body, without prejudging what that relation may be; it will suffice that for some reading of 'X' as the proper name of a man, it shall be correct to say that the mind is X's mind and the body is X's body. This notion of reincarnation is thus tied to our familiar notions of mind and body; and a discussion as to the possibility of reincarnation is an exercise in the analysis and logical mapping of those notions. Such a discussion, however, ought to interest others besides professional philosophers; for many philosophically unsophisticated people believe or half believe, or would like to believe, in reincarnation as thus understood. No doubt many of these people are silly or confused; but a main task of philosophy is to remove confusions. And even if a thesis is held by silly people for inadequate reasons, it may yet not be silly to examine it philosophically, if the thesis touches upon philosophically important matters.

I shall confine myself to the notion of reincarnation just explained; I shall not discuss metamorphosis or metempsychosis, whereby a mind might animate at different times a human and a non-human body. It is clear that to discuss this alleged possibility would involve all the problems of reincarnation, *plus* the further problems as to how we ought to talk about the minds and mental processes of the lower animals. Further, I shall stick to Western conceptions of mind and body whether on the part of philosophers or of others; I shall not try to discuss any Hindu or Buddhist views. This may strike some people as frivolous, in the way that it would be frivolous for somebody writing philosophical theology to discuss the writings of Judge Rutherford rather than of Thomas Aquinas. No doubt Hindu and Buddhist writings about reincarnation are of more inherent interest than *The Search for Bridey Murphy*; but I am wholly incompetent to discuss them; and even if I were myself able to talk about *atman* or *karma*, these are not notions which many of my readers could readily deploy. The vulgarized *Bridey Murphy* notion, on the other hand, is formulated in terms that we all use familiarly, even if confusedly; and if we discuss this notion, there is less chance of our darkening counsel with words void of understanding.

I have defined reincarnation in terms of the same mind's successively animating different bodies, and the question naturally arises whether, supposing e.g. that my mind once animated Julius Caesar's body, I could truly say that I was the *person* who crossed the Rubicon and said 'The die is cast'. Some philosophers, like Descartes and McTaggart, have held that it is all one whether we speak of the same mind or the same person. A slightly less strong thesis would be that at any rate if the same mind is still animating a human body there is the same person, even if there would not be the same person after metamorphosis into an insect or metempsychosis into a tree, and even if after becoming disembodied a human mind would not still be the same person. It seems clear, at any rate, that, assuming a human body continues to exist and to be animated by some human mind or other, there is the same person if and only if there is the same mind animating that body. Cases of multiple personality throw doubt on identity of person and identity of mind simultaneously; and apart from these cases I do not think we ever do feel serious doubts as to the identity either of person or of mind when we have to do with the same living human body.

2

It would thus be a natural extension of our existing usage, supposing that we found reason to say that in some cases the same mind successively animated different bodies, to say that in these cases there was the same person, and that this person's identity survived a change of body, as we know it can survive considerable physical changes within the lifetime of one body.

Anyhow, I am not going to retreat into what Professor Flew has aptly called a conventionalist sulk against such a way of talking. (He himself is surely indulging in just such a sulk when he says it is logically impossible for a person to survive death; for saying this only records a determination, though someone rose from the dead, not to *call* him the same person, or alternatively to go back on admitting he was dead.) I shall therefore assume henceforth that I am the same person as crossed the Rubicon and said 'The die is cast' if and only if my mind is the same mind as came to that bold decision; and I shall switch freely between speaking of the same mind and speaking of the same person. This of course does not mean that I propose to use the word 'mind' and 'person' indiscriminately; only that in my view, given a body, there is the same mind if and only if there is the same person.

The discussion will turn a great deal upon the relation between personal identity and memory. On the Lockean doctrine of personal identity, the question of reincarnation could be dealt with in short order; for, at any rate in the great majority of cases, a man has absolutely no memory of a previous existence; and if I do not remember a life previous to my present life, then on this theory the previous life must have been the life of a person different from me. But Locke's doctrine is quite indefensible. If a person is to remember truly what he did at an earlier date, it must already be true, before he turns his mind to the question what happened then, that the person who did the deed is the same person as the person who is now to be reminded of the matter; it cannot possibly be the case that the memory makes the person remembering to be the same person as the doer of the remembered deed.

Locke appealed to moral attitudes in support of his doctrine; he may fairly be said to have anticipated the ascriptivist doctrine of later Oxford philosophers, that the answer to a question 'Did he do it?' is not just a matter of fact but a matter for practical (legal or moral) decision. I have not much respect for this kind of view; but those with ascriptivist leanings would hardly now wish to say that the meaning of 'he', i.e. 'that person', in 'he did it' has moralistic overtones. The new-fangled ascriptivist view is that the verb 'did' has in certain contexts an *a*scriptive rather than *de*scriptive force, and it is not to our purpose to argue about that.

If I may declare my interest, Locke's view appears to me morally repugnant. We ought not to need a Freud to tell us that some men very readily forget their past misdeeds; I do not see why the possessors of such a convenient memory should be held the less responsible for what they have done—the mere fact of their being so constituted is often a sign of a vicious character. And even if a man's oblivion of a past misdeed is in itself wholly inculpable, his responsibility for the deed need not be diminished; a man who drives recklessly ought not to be excused by others or himself because he has forgotten the whole affair owing to concussion in the eventual crash. Perhaps Locke would think that God will hold such a man excused on Judgment Day; but I see no reason to think that.

If we reject Locke's doctrine, then surely it must already be significant, and possibly true, to say that I am the same person as decided to cross the Rubicon, regardless of whether I remember this or could remember this. The *prima facie* reason for thinking this would be somewhat as follows: I know very well what I mean by 'I'; very well then, I understand the propositions 'I lived in Rome before the Christian era', I decided to cross the Rubicon', etc., even if I have no memory of any such things. And could not such propositions be true?

McTaggart seriously attempts to make more of this hypothesis than an idle 'Why not?' He supposes that if the same mind passed immediately from animating one body to animating another, it would manifest in its new life abilities and traits of character developed in a past life; moreover, that if people had been friends or lovers in one life, their reincarnated minds would be so attuned to each other that if they met in the new life, a brief acquaintance would enable them to pick up the threads of the old relationship. It would be extremely difficult to collect supporting evidence; but on the face of it the hypothesis of such reincarnation is not wholly empty or out of touch with experiential facts; and McTaggart movingly argues that the prospect of it is something to give us hope and encouragement. Death does not then inevitably take away our hard-won gains in talent and virtue, nor the love of those dear to us; and the fear of losing memories, which often become burdensome, is outweighed by the hope that youth will return like the spring.

But do we after all understand the sort of first-person propositions of which the ones I just cited are illustrations? People may claim in all good faith to understand, and feel as though they understood, and yet turn out not to have understood; anyone who has to teach philosophy becomes well aware of this if he marks his own pupils' papers. And some sorts of pseudo-supposition give us a strong feeling of understanding in spite of gross incoherence: Wells's *The Time Machine* is none the less a 'convincing' story because there are three different and irreconcilable time-theories in the Time Traveller's opening remarks. Remarks about the general possibility of illusory understanding cannot of course themselves throw doubt upon a specific claim to understand a proposition; any more than general reflections about the possibility of hallucination ought to make me feel some slight doubt as to whether I am reading this paper. The reason why we need to remind ourselves of the possibility of illusory understanding is rather that, when faced by specific arguments that would show an alleged understanding to be only illusory, we may be tempted not to look for a flaw in the arguments but just to reiterate that we do understand; and that isn't good enough.

What do I mean by propositions containing the word

'I'? If I enunciate such propositions to hearers or readers, they will be given certain information, true or false, about the speaker or writer: they will be truly informed, since the speaker or writer in question is Peter Geach, if and only if the corresponding proposition is true that they would enunciate using 'Peter Geach' where I use 'I' and making the requisite grammatical changes. But if this were the only use of the word 'I', then propositions like 'I crossed the Rubicon' would be significant indeed, but also straight-forwardly refutable; for the man Peter Geach never did so. Even if the man Peter Geach is the same person as the man Julius Caesar, they are certainly different men; they were for example born at different times to a different pair of parents.

The only interpretation of 'I' for which such first-person propositions would not be straightforwardly refutable is a certain soliloquistic use of 'I'. By way of illustrating this, consider a Descartes brooding over his German stove and saying, 'I'm getting into a frightful puzzle—but what then is this "I" that is puzzled?' Or again, McTaggart says to himself, 'I have a pain—but then I should not be justified in saying this unless it were also justifiable to say that one and the same self both has a pain and judges himself to have a pain; and how could this be justifiable unless I, the self in question, could directly perceive myself as both having the pain and forming the judgment?'

This sort of philosophizing is now rather old-fashioned, but it is still worth while to see what its purport is and what is wrong with it—particularly as some recent statements and refutations of the Descartes–McTaggart thesis are gravely misleading. The use of 'I' here is essentially soliloquistic; the idea is that each man who has mastered the use of 'I' could in solitude use these lines of argument to convince himself. It might seem superfluous to explain that this is the point of the argument, but I am afraid it is necessary in reply to some misunderstandings. For example, in what professes to be a discussion of Descartes, Professor Passmore has considered whether one person can refute another who says 'I do not think', or need believe another who says 'I do think'; he appears quite unaware that this was not at all Descartes' point.

Again, Descartes and McTaggart were not trying to prove a conclusion to be necessary, or its denial to be logically self-contradictory, but simply to give each of us a way of reaching an absolutely indubitable truth. Many people have been convinced that no empirical truth *is* absolutely indubitable; but Descartes and McTaggart did not think so, and it is just a misinterpretation to argue that they must have been trying to establish a truth as logically necessary because they tried to establish it as indubitable.

But what is it that is indubitable? What are the soliloquistic utterances 'I am in horrible pain' and 'I am frightfully puzzled' supposed to supply over and above the soliloquistic utterances 'This pain is horrible' and 'This is frightfully puzzling'? Descartes and McTaggart plainly supposed that here we had indubitable answers to the questions 'Who is in horrible pain?' and 'Who is being frightfully puzzled?' But the sense of a 'Who?' question is surely fixed by the range of acceptable answers; and here we have no idea what the range of the answers is allowed to be —we know only that the proper names of ordinary life are not acceptable answers, since they relate to human beings and not to Cartesian egos or McTaggart's 'selves'.

People who are inclined to accept the Descartes–McTaggart thesis would often follow McTaggart in finding it self-evident that a self, or what each of us means by the soliloquistic 'I', has no matter in its make-up—which is certainly not true of human beings. It appears to me that this 'self-evident truth' amounts to no more than a stipulation; no mention of a thing with matter in its make-up is to *count* as an answer, when the soliloquist asks, as regards his own pain or puzzlement, who it is that is in pain or puzzled. We are then left with a question where ordinary sense has been excluded by excluding the ordinary answers to it; failing a new stipulation of a set of admissible answers, the question then has no sense, and we ought not to look for an answer.

Descartes indeed did not just say it was self-evident that 'I' used soliloquistically had an immaterial reference; this conclusion was supposed to follow from the premises, as regards each one of us, that for no material thing is it beyond his power to doubt its existence, and that for what he means by 'I' it is beyond his power to doubt its existence. But this reasoning is patently fallacious. It is in fact the same fallacy as the notorious old Larvatus or Masked Man fallacy: was it, perhaps, by a Freudian self-betrayal that Descartes wrote in his private notebook '*larvatus prodeo*', 'I come forward in a mask'? If the masked man is somebody whose identity I don't know, and my father is not someone whose identity I don't know, it does not follow that the masked man is not my father, but only that I do not know him to be my father. Similarly, if a man can bring himself to doubt whether anything material exists, but cannot bring himself to doubt his own existence, the existence of what he means by the soliloquistic 'I', then all that follows is that in this state of doubt he does not know that he himself is a material being, not that he is not one.

It appears to me that this use of 'I' in soliloquy is a degenerate use, and there is no question of its referring to anything. The word 'degenerate' is not here a term of abuse; I am using it much as mathematicians do. They call '$0 . x^2 + 3x - 6 = 0$' a degenerate quadratic equation, because in solving it you ignore the term with 'x^2' in it, and do not apply the general rule for solving quadratics, but simply solve '$3x - 6 = 0$'. In the sort of soliloquistic utterances I have mentioned, 'I', the apparent subject-term, often cancels out in much the same way.

In communication with others, a man uses 'I' in expressing his mental states in order that others may learn who is in pain or puzzled or what not; it is natural that he should still use 'I' in soliloquy when expressing these states, but his 'I' has not now the role of telling *himself* who is in pain or puzzled. It no longer refers to a person or a human being; just as 'there' in 'there is a difference between pride and vanity' has no longer the role of referring to a place; or

again, the '*es*' in the German idiom '*es gibt*' (corresponding
to 'there is': literally 'it gives') no longer refers to a giver.

I do not mean that 'I' in soliloquy *cannot* refer to the person speaking. If Descartes had asked 'Who am I?' because
he had lost his memory, 'I' would have referred to Descartes
—but just on that account 'I am René Descartes' would
have been an answer he could give himself when he recovered
his memory. And this sort of answer does not suit the sense
he was in fact trying to give the question, or rather, does
not suit his requirements as to what the sense should be,
for I do not admit that any sense answering to his requirements can be given to the question. Again, if Descartes had
heard himself groaning 'I am in terrible pain', he might have
been in such an abnormal state of mind as to want to know
who was meant by 'I', because he did not know who had
groaned; but again 'René Descartes' would be the right
answer, though unlikely in the circumstances to be a helpful
one.

This last remark of mine might be doubted, because of
cases of multiple personality. In the case I have just given,
Descartes might be a victim of this disorder; the groan
'I am in pain' might come from the personality Denys
Récartes, while the personality René Descartes wondered
who it was that was in pain. Then our puzzle as to the range
of allowable answers to the question 'Who then is in pain?'
might perhaps thus be resolved: in the soliloquistic use, 'I'
would refer not to a person as hitherto understood but to a
personality, and the relevant answers to the question would
consist in mention of or reference to some personality or
other.

The question which mental acts and experiences count as
belonging to the same personality would be a rather difficult
one to tackle: and I do not propose to tackle it. I shall
assume, for the sake of argument, that psychiatrists have
devised some reasonably coherent and workable criterion
of identity for personalities. Even if we assume this, and
assume that the soliloquistic 'I' relates to a personality, this
would not enable us to make sense of the proposition 'I

decided to cross the Rubicon', said by me now. For then that personality of the man Julius Caesar to which is attributable the decision to cross the Rubicon would have to be identified as one and the same personality with that personality of the man Peter Geach which devised the present argument. Psychiatrists have certainly not devised any criterion of identity for personalities clear enough to enable us to make such identifications, or even to say what they would amount to; therefore such identifications so far make no sense.

Incidentally, the possibilities of multiple personality spoil the resort to the *Cogito* as an irrefragable certitude. In a novel of Helen Nielsen's the 'I' of the story is told by the automatic writing of his own hand that he is only a secondary personality produced by stress; which suggests the doubt 'Perhaps I am not a substantive person, but only a pathological condition'—a rather worse suspicion than that one is only a thing in somebody's dream. Unlike Descartes' demon, the conditions that would give rise to such doubt do actually exist.

In view of all this, we cannot regard the *Cogito* as giving us a ready access to an identifiable immaterial somewhat that might conceivably survive transference from one body to another. Even if mental illnesses were infectious, one that A caught from B could hardly be regarded as an individual entity which persisted through the transference from A to B, like a microbe physically transferred; and a 'personality' might have only the sort of identity that an illness has.

If the preceding arguments are sound, my present self-consciousness cannot avail to give me an understanding of such propositions as 'I lived before the Christian era', 'I decided to cross the Rubicon', etc. (There is of course a sense in which these propositions would relate in the ordinary way to the man Peter Geach, who was born in 1916 and has never seen the Rubicon; and then they are straightforward empirical falsehoods.) But it might be supposed that memory would make all the difference. If it were not a matter just of my suppositionally extending the use of 'I' to the life of Julius Caesar, but of my ostensibly remembering as my own doings episodes in the life of Julius Caesar, then surely there could be no doubt as to the significance of such first-person past-tense propositions when I uttered them; surely then I should not be just mouthing words. And if my ostensible memories turned out, e.g. to clear up historical puzzles about the life of Julius Caesar in a satisfactory way, then would there not be even good empirical evidence that I was the same person as Julius Caesar? Might not such a conclusion become as well-grounded as many other empirical conclusions, so that it would be almost inevitable to accept it if one did not lapse into a conventionalist sulk?

To avoid the suspicion of such a lapse, I shall not take the short way with someone thus appealing to a supposed memory—namely, that if a proposition 'p' has no significance for me, neither can 'I remember that p' have significance for me. I think this short way is sound, but undeniably there is some appearance of a trick, and I do not know how to allay such doubt. Instead, I shall try to discuss the concept of memory on its own account. Here I cannot claim to give a correct account or analysis of the concept, only to remind you of some truths and expose some errors; and nevertheless I hope to show that memory could in no case give content to an idea of reincarnation.

Not all memories are to be accepted; some recollections are trustworthy, others not. This truism is often evaded by a conventionalist sulk—by refusing to *call* anything a memory, or to *say* that somebody remembered, unless the memory is veridical. This sometimes goes with a pretended appeal to linguistic usage—it is alleged, e.g. by Moore, that we *don't say* 'memory' or 'remembers' except with the implication that things happened as remembered. Of course we in fact constantly say that a man's memory is bad or mistaken, that he remembers things wrong, etc. I have not bothered to look this up in the dictionary; if the dictionary says otherwise, so much the worse for the dictionary.

Next, there is no inner self-authenticating sign by which to sort out memory-knowledge from possibly erroneous memory-belief; and if there were such a sign, it would be no use. For my memory sometimes deceives me, even when I have no doubt as to what happened. What if there is a sign by the absence of which I could have told this unreliable memory-belief from memory-knowledge? Since no doubt was raised at the time, I was unable to make any use of this fact that the sign was absent; and it is cold comfort to be told afterwards by a follower of Cook Wilson, 'You didn't *know* the thing had happened, you only *took it for granted*'. The rejection of the internal sign does not lead to scepticism; as Hume says, we can no more help judging than breathing, and we shall continue to form some unhesitating judgments as to our past life; and though some of these will be mistaken, many will not.

I have just been taking it for granted that there are episodic memory-judgments—that the noun 'memory' and the verb 'remember' do not relate only to the continued possession of capacities. I should say, as I did in my book *Mental Acts*, that there is an episodic act of judgment at least as often as a man is faced with a question, and answers it with consideration; in this sense, it seems clear that there are *inter alia* memory-judgments. I think I need not discuss arguments to the contrary, except for one, to which Professor Ayer has given some countenance. Ayer sketches a doctrine of memory somewhat reminiscent of Austin's theory of knowledge; 'in claiming to remember, one is not so much describing one's present state of mind as giving an assurance that the event occurred, at the same time implying that one is in a position to know that it occurred'.[1]

Like Austin's theory, Ayer's theory takes into account only a tiny fragment of the usage of the verb; namely, its use in assertoric first-person sentences of the present tense. Austin obviously supposed that once one had given a performatory analysis of such sentences, the task of accounting for other uses of the verbs concerned would take care of itself. It would however be absurd to say, for example, that in the proposition 'When the cock crew, Peter remembered what his Master had said' there is no reference to an episodic

[1] *The Problem of Knowledge*, Penguin Books, p. 147.

experience of Peter's; and if such references to episodic experiences cannot be eliminated by theories in a performatory style, we cannot attach any importance to the alleged elimination in the first-person present-tense case.

Even for assertoric first-person sentences, Ayer's theory breaks down. An argument of the form 'I remember so-and-so, and if I remember so-and-so I must have been alive in such a year, so I was alive in such a year' is an ordinary valid *modus ponens*, and its validity requires that 'I remember so-and-so' should be a *bona fide* proposition; that is, a proposition whose sense is unaffected by its now occurring as an *if* clause and now getting asserted on its own account. (These obvious logical objections may of course be readily adapted to serve against Austin's theory.)

All the same, the occurrence in someone of an episodic judgment that he himself did or underwent so-and-so is not a sufficient condition for his having then and there *remembered* that he did or underwent so-and-so. If a man's judgment is consciously based on inference, or on accepting the testimony of others that he did so-and-so, we should unhesitatingly deny that it was a memory-judgment. (This would *not* be because some sort of memory-tone was absent from the episode of judging; for, as I argued, there *is* no special experience that occurs when and only when we are remembering, as opposed to just judging about, the past.) Perhaps the man himself is unaware that the reason why he thinks so-and-so happened is that somebody told him, or again unaware that he has simply concluded that it *must* have happened; nevertheless, if *we* have good reason to suppose that this is why he thinks it, we shall not unhesitatingly admit that he remembered; if we do say he remembered, we shall be putting 'remembered' so to speak in scare-quotes. Similarly, if the only reason why a man 'remembered' something was that a hypnotist had given him a post-hypnotic suggestion that he would 'remember' it.

In saying that a man not merely judges but remembers that something happened in the past, we are not, I argued, committing ourselves to the assertion that the thing did happen; but we are saying something about the provenance of his present impression as to how things happened. In some ways the concept of memory is like that of a photograph of someone. A photograph, or a memory, may be so confused that you cannot say it's a photograph, or memory, of X at all. But a blurred photograph of X is a genuine photograph of X, whereas a clear photograph of X's twin brother, though it may give you a much better idea of what X looks like, isn't a photograph of X at all. I am not competent to fill out this part of the analysis of memory; but fortunately what I have said will suffice.

For let us suppose that after a period of unconsciousness I wake up to find myself the helpless prisoner of a ruthless surgeon. He tells me that I am going to be dissected and my *disjecta membra* used for future experiments; but not to worry, for my whole life's memories have been got out of me by a truth-drug while I was unconscious and will be fed into the previously washed brain of another victim. It seems to me that the powers that the surgeon claims are only conceivable extensions of existing techniques. 'Memories' can be produced by hypnosis; tampering with the brain might erase all a man's genuine memories as concussion sometimes does; and the use of truth-drugs I have supposed would just mean doing on a large scale what can certainly be done on a small scale. So I hope I have not myself fallen into the trap of producing in myself a spurious understanding of a really incoherent story—a trap, I have argued, that yawns for all who use fantasy in philosophy.

Well, if the surgeon's claims did make coherent sense, we may suppose them to be true: then ought I to take his advice not to worry, on the score that I shall live on in the body to which my 'memories' are transferred? It seems to me (as I am, not as I then might be) that I shall have every reason to worry; for if my mind survived the dissection at all, it would not at any rate survive in the clean-washed brain stuffed with 'memories' of my life. The provenance of these 'memories' would be so different from the provenance of unquestionably genuine memories that they could not be counted as memories.

The other victim might claim *bona fide* to be Peter Geach; but he wouldn't be Peter Geach, and God knows what would have happened to Peter Geach.

Recollect that *ex hypothesi* the other victim's claim to be Peter Geach would have the same grounds even if I were rescued after the surgeon had brain-washed him. Now in this case he *couldn't* be Peter Geach. So, since he would have no better claim to be Peter Geach if I were murdered, he *would not* be Peter Geach even in that case.

If I am right about the mad-surgeon case, the mere fact that somebody claimed to remember episodes in Julius Caesar's life as episodes in his own life would not give us the least reason to believe that he was the same person as Julius Caesar. Even if his alleged memories—apart from the claim of personal identity—turned out to give us convincing and reliable information about the life of Caesar, this would only help historians interested in Caesar, not philosophers or others interested in reincarnation. For there would be no way of removing the doubt as to whether the claim of these 'memories' to be memories is vitiated by their provenance; and if they are thus vitiated at their origin, they are no more evidence of personal identity than the surgeon's other victim's claim to be Peter Geach would go to show that he really was Peter Geach.

Even if the alleged memories related to things that 'only Julius Caesar can have known', the case for reincarnation would be stronger. For our ordinary beliefs as to what 'only so-and-so can have known' are based on well-founded generalizations as to the limits of human knowledge. Regarding cases that would constitute exceptions to such generalizations, it is absurdly inconsistent to make inferences still using a premise that 'Only so-and-so can have known that'. There is a well-known story in psychical research that ought to show the fallacy of such inferences. A medium gave a sitter touching and convincing 'messages' as from the spirit of a dead friend, including things that 'only he can have known'; but the friend turned out to have been alive and in a normal state of mind at the time of the 'messages'.

I conclude that the *Bridey Murphy* idea of reincarnation not only is generally held for no good reason, but could barely be supplied with good reason, or even with clear sense. This result is not very surprising, nor of itself very interesting; but I hope the way I have taken to this conclusion has passed through some philosophically fertile patches.

2

Immortality

Everybody knows that men die, and though most of us have read the advertisement 'Millions now living will never die', it is commonly believed that every man born will some day die; yet historically many men have believed that there is a life after death, and indeed that this after-life will never end. That is: there has been a common belief both in *survival* of bodily death and in *immortality*. Now a philosopher might interest himself specially in immortality, as opposed to survival; conceding survival for the sake of argument, he might raise and examine conceptual difficulties about *endless* survival. But the question of immortality cannot even arise unless men do survive bodily death; and, as we shall see, there are formidable difficulties even about survival. It is these difficulties I shall be discussing, not the special ones about endless survival.

There are various views as to the character of the after-life. One view is that man has a subtle, ordinarily invisible, body which survives the death of the ordinary gross body. This view has a long history, and seems to be quite popular in England at the moment. So far as I can see, the view is open to no philosophical objection, but likewise wholly devoid of philosophical interest; the mind-body problem must after all be just the same for an ethereal body as for a gross one. There could clearly be no philosophical reasons for belief in such subtle bodies, but only empirical ones; such reasons are in fact alleged, and we are urged to study the evidence.

Philosophy can at this point say something: about what sort of evidence would be required. The existence of subtle bodies is a matter within the purview of physical science; evidence for it should satisfy such criteria of existence as physicists use, and should refer not only to what people say they have seen, heard, and felt, but also to effects produced by subtle bodies on physicists' apparatus. The believer in 'subtle bodies' must, I think, accept the physicist's criteria of existence; there would surely be a conceptual muddle in speaking of 'bodies' but saying they might be incapable of affecting any physical apparatus. For what distinguishes real physical objects from hallucinations, even collective hallucinations, is that physical objects act on one another, and do so in just the same way whether they are being observed or not; this is the point, I think, at which a pheno-menalist account of physical objects breaks down. If, there-fore, 'subtle bodies' produce no physical effects, they are not bodies at all.

How is it, then, that 'subtle bodies' have never forced themselves upon the attention of physicists, as X-rays did, by spontaneous interference with physical apparatus? There are supposed to be a lot of 'subtle bodies' around, and physicists have a lot of delicate apparatus; yet physicists not engaged in psychical research are never bothered by the interference of 'subtle bodies'. In the circumstances I think it wholly irrational to believe in 'subtle bodies'. Moreover, when I who am no physicist am invited to study the evi-dence for 'subtle bodies', I find that very fact suspicious. The discoverers of X-rays and electrons did not appeal to the lay public, but to physicists, to study the evidence; and so long as physicists (at least in general) refuse to take 'subtle bodies' seriously, a study of evidence for them by a layman like myself would be a waste of time.

When *philosophers* talk of life after death, what they mostly have in mind is a doctrine that may be called Platonic —it is found in its essentials in the *Phaedo*. It may be briefly stated thus: 'Each man's make-up includes a wholly im-material thing, his mind and soul. It is the mind that sees and hears and feels and thinks and chooses—in a word, is conscious. The mind is the person; the body is extrinsic to the person, like a suit of clothes. Though body and mind affect one another, the mind's existence is quite independent of the body's; and there is thus no reason why the mind should not go on being conscious indefinitely after the death of the body, and even if it never again has with any body that sort of connexion which it now has.

This Platonic doctrine has a strong appeal, and there are plausible arguments in its favour. It appears a clearly intelligible supposition that I should go on after death having the same sorts of experience as I now have, even if I then have no body at all. For although these experiences are connected with processes in the body—sight, for example, with processes in the eyes, optic nerves, and brain —nevertheless there is no necessity of thought about the connexion—it is easy to conceive of someone who has no eyes having the experience called sight. He would be having the same experience as I who have eyes do, and I know what sort of experience that is because I have the experience.

Let us now examine these arguments. When a word can be used to stand for a private experience, like the words 'seeing' or 'pain', it is certainly tempting to suppose that the giving these words a meaning is itself a private experience— indeed that they get their meaning just from the experiences they stand for. But this is really nonsense: if a sentence I hear or utter contains the word 'pain', do I help myself to grasp its sense by giving myself a pain? Might not this be, on the contrary, rather distracting? As Wittgenstein said, to think you get the concept of pain by having a pain is like thinking you get the concept of a minus quantity by running up an overdraft. Our concepts of seeing, hearing, pain, anger, etc., apply in the first instance to human beings; we willingly extend them (say) to cats, dogs, and horses, but we rightly feel uncomfortable about extending them to very alien creatures and speaking of a slug's hearing or an angry ant. Do we know at all what it would be to apply such concepts to an immaterial being? I think not.

One may indeed be tempted to evade difficulties by saying: 'An immaterial spirit is angry or in pain if it feels *the same way* as I do when I am angry or in pain'. But, as Wittgenstein remarked, this is just like saying: 'Of course I know what it is for the time on the Sun to be five o'clock: it's five o'clock on the Sun at the very moment when it's five o'clock here!'—which plainly gets us no forrader. If there is a difficulty in passing from 'I am in pain' or 'Smith is in pain' to 'an immaterial spirit is in pain', there is equally a difficulty in passing from 'Smith feels the same way as I do' to 'an immaterial spirit feels the same way as I do'.

In fact, the question is, whether a private experience does suffice, as is here supposed, to a give a meaning to a psychological verb like 'to see'. I am not trying to throw doubt on there being private experiences; of course men have thoughts they do not utter and pains they do not show; of course I may see something without any behaviour to show I see it; nor do I mean to emasculate these propositions with neo-behaviourist dialectics. But it is not a question of whether seeing is (sometimes) a private experience, but whether one can attach meaning to the verb 'to see' by a private uncheckable performance; and this is what I maintain one cannot do to any word at all.

One way to show that a word's being given a meaning cannot be a private uncheckable performance is the following: We can take a man's word for it that a linguistic expression has given him some private experience—e.g. has revived a painful memory, evoked a visual image, or given him a thrill in the pit of the stomach. But we cannot take his word for it that he attached a sense to the expression, even if we accept his *bona fides*; for later events may convince us that in fact he attached no sense to the expression. Attaching sense to an expression is thus not to be identified with any private experience that accompanies the expression; and I have argued this, not by attacking the idea of private experiences, but by contrasting the attaching of sense to an expression with some typical private experiences that may be connected with the expression.

We give words a sense—whether they are psychological words like 'seeing' and 'pain', or other words—by getting into a way of using them; and though a man can invent for himself a way of using a word, it must be a way that other people *could* follow—otherwise we are back to the idea of conferring meaning by a private uncheckable performance. Well, how do we eventually use such words as 'see', 'hear', 'feel', when we have got into the way of using them? We do not exercise these concepts only so as to pick our cases of seeing and the rest in our separate worlds of sense-experience; on the contrary, these concepts are used in association with a host of other concepts relating, e.g., to the physical characteristics of what is seen and the behaviour of those who do see. In saying this I am not putting forward a theory, but just reminding you of very familiar features in the everyday use of the verb 'to see' and related expressions; our ordinary talk about seeing would cease to be intelligible if there were cut out of it such expressions as 'I can't see, it's too far off', 'I caught his eye', 'Don't look round', etc. Do not let the bogy of behaviourism scare you off observing these features; I am not asking you to believe that 'to see' is itself a word for a kind of behaviour. But the concept of seeing can be maintained only because it has threads of connexion with these other non-psychological concepts; break enough threads, and the concept of seeing collapses.

We can now see the sort of difficulties that arise if we try to apply concepts like *seeing* and *feeling* to disembodied spirits. Let me give an actual case of a psychological concept's collapsing when its connexions were broken. Certain hysterics claimed to have a magnetic sense; it was discovered, however, that their claim to be having magnetic sensations did not go with the actual presence of a magnet in their environment, but only with their belief that a magnet was present. Psychologists did not now take the line: We may take the patients' word for it that they have peculiar sensations—only the term 'magnetic sensations' has proved inappropriate, as having been based on a wrong causal hypothesis. On the contrary, patients' reports of magnetic sensations were thenceforward written off as being among the odd things that hysterical patients sometimes say. Now far fewer of the ordinary connexions of a sensation-concept were broken here than would be broken if we tried to apply a sensation-concept like seeing to a disembodied spirit.

If we conclude that the ascription of sensations and feelings to a disembodied spirit does not make sense, it does not obviously follow, as you might think, that we must deny the possibility of disembodied spirits altogether. Aquinas for example was convinced that there are disembodied spirits but ones that cannot see or hear or feel pain or fear or anger; he allowed them no mental operations except those of thought and will. Damned spirits would suffer from frustration of their evil will, but not from aches and pains or foul odours or the like. It would take me too far to discuss whether his reasons for thinking this were good; I want to show what follows from this view. In our human life thinking and choosing are intricately bound up with a play of sensations and mental images and emotions; if after a lifetime of thinking and choosing in this human way there is left only a disembodied mind whose thought is wholly non-sensuous and whose rational choices are unaccompanied by any human feelings—can we still say there remains the same person? Surely not: such a soul is not the person who died but a mere remnant of him. And this is just what Aquinas says (in his commentary on I Corinthians 15): *anima mea non est ego*, my soul is not I; and if only souls are saved, *I* am not saved, nor is any man. If some time after Peter Geach's death there is again a man identifiable as Peter Geach, then Peter Geach again, or still, lives: otherwise not.

Though a surviving mental remnant of a person, preserving some sort of physical continuity with the man you knew, would not be Peter Geach, this does not show that such a measure of survival is not possible; but its possibility does raise serious difficulties, even if such dehumanized thinking and willing is really conceivable at all. For *whose* thinking would this be? Could we tell whether *one* or *many* disembodied spirits thought the thoughts in question?

We touch here on the old problem: what constitutes there being two disembodied minds (at the same time, that is)? Well, what constitutes there being two pennies? It may happen that one penny is bent and corroded while another is in mint condition; but such differences cannot be what make the two pennies to be two—the two pennies could not have these varied fortunes if they were not already distinct. In the same way, differences of memories or of aims could not constitute the difference between two disembodied minds, but could only supervene upon a difference already existing. What does constitute the difference between two disembodied human minds? If we could find no ground of differentiation, then not only would that which survived be a mere remnant of a person—there would not even be a surviving individuality.

Could we say that souls are different because in the first instance they were souls of different bodies, and then remain different on that account when they are no longer embodied? I do not think this solution would do at all if differentiation by reference to different bodies were merely retrospective. It might be otherwise if we held, with Aquinas, that the relation to a body was not merely retrospective—that each disembodied human soul permanently retained a capacity for reunion to such a body as would reconstitute a man identifiable with the man who died. This might satisfactorily account for the individuation of disembodied human souls; they would differ by being fitted for reunion to different bodies; but it would entail that the possibility of disembodied human souls stood or fell with the *possibility* of a dead man's living again *as a man*.

Some Scholastics held that just as two pennies or two cats differ by being different bits of matter, so human souls differ by containing different 'spiritual matter'. Aquinas regarded this idea as self-contradictory; it is at any rate much too obscure to count as establishing a possibility of distinct disembodied souls. Now this recourse to 'spiritual matter' might well strike us merely as the filling of a conceptual lacuna with a nonsensical piece of jargon. But it is not only

Scholastic philosophers who assimilate mental processes to physical ones, only thinking of mental processes as taking place in an *immaterial* medium; and many people think it easy to conceive of distinct disembodied souls because they are illegitimately ascribing to souls a sort of differentiation— say, by existing *side by side*—that can be significantly ascribed only to bodies. The same goes for people who talk about souls as being 'fused' or 'merged' in a Great Soul; they are imagining some such change in the world of souls as occurs to a drop of water falling into a pool or to a small lump of wax that is rubbed into a big one. Now if only people *talked* about 'spiritual matter', instead of just thinking in terms of it unawares, their muddle could be more easily detected and treated.

To sum up what I have said so far: The possibility of life after death for Peter Geach appears to stand or fall with the possibility of there being once again a man identifiable as Peter Geach. The existence of a disembodied soul would not be a survival of the person Peter Geach; and even in such a truncated form, individual existence seems to require at least a persistent possibility of the soul's again entering into the make-up of a man who is identifiably Peter Geach.

This suggests a form of belief in survival that seems to have become quite popular of late in the West—at any rate as a half-belief—namely, the belief in reincarnation. Could it in fact have a clear sense to say that a baby born in Oxford this year is Hitler living again?

How could it be shown that the Oxford baby was Hitler? Presumably by memories and similarities of character. I maintain that no amount of such evidence would make it reasonable to identify the baby as Hitler. Similarities of character are of themselves obviously insufficient. As regards memories: If on growing up the Oxford baby reveals knowledge of what we should ordinarily say only Hitler can have known, does this establish a presumption that the child is Hitler? Not at all. In normal circumstances we know when to say 'only he can have known that'; when queer things start happening, we have no right to stick to our ordinary assumptions as to what can be known. And suppose that for some time the child 'is' Hitler by our criteria, and later on 'is' Goering? or might not several children simultaneously satisfy the criteria for 'being' Hitler?

These are not merely captious theoretical objections. Spirit-mediums, we are told, will in trance convincingly enact the part of various people: sometimes of fictitious characters, like Martians, or Red Indians ignorant of Red Indian languages, or the departed 'spirits' of Johnny Walker and John Jamieson; there are even stories of mediums' giving convincing 'messages' from people who were alive and normally conscious at the time of the 'message'. Now a medium giving messages from the dead is not said to be the dead man, but rather to be controlled by his spirit. What then can show whether the Oxford child 'is' Hitler or is merely 'controlled' by Hitler's spirit? For all these reasons the appearance that there might be good evidence for reincarnation dissolves on a closer view.[1]

Nor do I see, for that matter, how the mental phenomena of mediumship could ever make it reasonable to believe that a human soul survived and communicated. For someone to carry on in a dramatic way quite out of his normal character is a common hysterical symptom; so if a medium does this in a trance, it is no evidence of anything except an abnormal condition of the medium's own mind. As for the medium's telling us things that 'only the dead can have known', I repeat that in these queer cases we have no right to stick to our ordinary assumptions about what can be known. Moreover, as I said, there are cases, as well-authenticated as any, in which the medium convincingly enacted the part of X and told things that 'Only X could have known' when X was in fact alive and normally conscious, so that his soul was certainly not trying to communicate by way of the medium! Even if we accept all the queer stories of spirit-messages, the result is only to open up a vast field of queer possibilities—not in the least to force us to say that mediums were possessed by such-and-such souls. This was argued

[1] Cf. Essay I for further development of these arguments.

by Bradley long ago in his essay 'The Evidences of Spiritualism', and he has never been answered.

How could a living man be rightly identifiable with a man who previously died? Let us first consider our normal criteria of personal identity. When we say an old man is the same person as the baby born seventy years before, we believe that the old man has material continuity with the baby. Of course this is not a criterion in the sense of being what we judge identity by; for the old man will not have been watched for seventy years continuously, even by rota! But something we regarded as disproving the material continuity (e.g. absence of a birthmark, different fingerprints) would disprove personal identity. Further, we believe that material continuity establishes a one–one relation: one baby grows up into one old man, and one old man has grown out of one baby. (Otherwise there would have to be at some stage a drastic change, a fusion or fission, which we should regard as destroying personal identity.) Moreover, the baby-body never coexists with the aged body, but develops into it.

Now it seems to me that we cannot rightly identify a man living 'again' with a man who died unless *material* conditions of identity are fulfilled. There must be some one–one relation of material continuity between the old body and the new. I am not saying that the new body need be even in part materially *identical* with the old; this, unlike material continuity, is not required for personal identity, for the old man need not have kept even a grain of matter from the baby of seventy years ago.

We must here notice an important fallacy. I was indicating just now that I favour Aquinas's doctrine that two coexisting souls differ by being related to two different bodies and that two coexisting human bodies, like two pennies or two cats, differ by being different bits of matter. Well, if it is difference of matter that makes two bodies different, it may seem to follow that a body can maintain its identity only if at least some identifiable matter remains in it all the time; otherwise it is no more the same body than the wine in a cask that is continuously emptied and refilled is the same wine. But just this is the fallacy: it does not follow, if difference in a certain respect at a certain time suffices to show non-identity, that sameness in that respect over a period of time is necessary to identity. Thus, Sir John Cutler's famous pair of stockings were the same pair all the time, although they started as silk and by much mending ended as worsted; people have found it hard to see this, because if at a given time there is a silk pair and also a worsted pair then there are two pairs. Again, it is clear that the same man may be in Birmingham at noon and in Oxford at 7 p.m., even though a man in Birmingham and a man in Oxford at a given time must be two different men. Once formulated, the fallacy is obvious, but it might be deceptive if not formulated.

'Why worry even about material continuity? Would not mental continuity be both necessary and sufficient?' Necessary, but not sufficient. Imagine a new 'Tichborne' trial. The claimant knows all the things he ought to know, and talks convincingly to the long-lost heir's friends. But medical evidence about scars and old fractures and so on indicates that he cannot be the man; moreover, the long-lost heir's corpse is decisively identified at an exhumation. Such a case would bewilder us, particularly if the claimant's *bona fides* were manifest. (He might, for example, voluntarily take a lie-detecting test.) But we should certainly not allow the evidence of mental connexions with the long-lost heir to settle the matter in the claimant's favour: the claimant cannot be the long-lost heir, whose body we know lies buried in Australia, and if he honestly thinks he is then we must try to cure him of a delusion.

'But if I went on being conscious, why should I worry which body I have?' To use the repeated 'I' prejudges the issue; a fairer way of putting the point would be: If there is going to be a consciousness that includes ostensible memories of my life, why should I worry about which body this consciousness goes with? When we put it that way, it is quite easy to imagine circumstances in which one would worry—particularly if the ostensible memories of my life

27

were to be produced by processes that can produce entirely spurious memories.[1]

If, however, memory is not enough for personal identity; if a man's living again does involve some bodily as well as mental continuity with the man who lived formerly; then we might fairly call his new bodily life a resurrection. So the upshot of our whole argument is that unless a man comes to life again by resurrection, he does not live again after death. At best some mental remnant of him would survive death; and I should hold that the possibility even of such survival involves at least a permanent *capacity* for renewed human life; if reincarnation is excluded, this means: a capacity for resurrection. It may be hard to believe in the resurrection of the body: but Aquinas argued in his commentary on I Corinthians 15, which I have already cited, that it is much harder to believe in an immortal but permanently disembodied human soul; for that would mean believing that a soul, whose very identity depends on the capacity for reunion with one human body rather than another, will continue to exist for ever with this capacity unrealized.

Speaking of the resurrection, St. Paul used the simile of a seed that is planted and grows into an ear of corn, to show the relation between the corpse and the body that rises again from the dead. This simile fits in well enough with our discussion. In this life, the bodily aspect of personal identity requires a one–one relationship and material continuity; one baby body grows into one old man's body by a continuous process. Now similarly there is a one–one relationship between the buried seed and the ear that grows out of it; one seed grows into one ear, one ear comes from one seed; and the ear of corn is materially continuous with the seed but need not have any material identity with it.

There is of course no philosophical reason to expect that from a human corpse there will arise at some future date a new human body, continuous in some way with the corpse; and in some particular cases there appear strong empirical objections. But apart from the *possibility* of resurrection, it

[1] Cf. the example of the mad surgeon's procedures in Essay 1.

seems to me a mere illusion to have any hope for life after death. I am of the mind of Judas Maccabeus: if there is no resurrection, it is superfluous and vain to pray for the dead.

The traditional faith of Christianity, inherited from Judaism, is that at the end of this age Messiah will come and men rise from their graves to die no more. That faith is not going to be shaken by inquiries about bodies burned to ashes or eaten by beasts; those who might well suffer just such death in martyrdom were those who were most confident of a glorious reward in the resurrection. One who shares that hope will hardly wish to take out an occultistic or philosophical insurance policy, to guarantee some sort of survival as an annuity, in case God's promise of resurrection should fail.

3

What Do We Think With?

I wrote this paper because I was asked to contribute to a
dialogue between materialists and anti-materialists. It was
proposed to me that I should speak in defence of the soul;
but meditation on titles with the word 'soul' in them did not
start me thinking to any good effect. I finally proposed the
title I have just given, because it marks a fairly clear division
between materialist and anti-materialist views. Materialists
would say that each of us thinks with a material part of himself; specifically, with some tract of the brain—for there
is no other part of the body that we have the least reason
to regard as an organ of thought. I am an anti-materialist.
One form of anti-materialism is immaterialism—the view
that each of us thinks with an immaterial part of him, his
mind or soul. I shall examine immaterialism later; for the
moment let me just point out that materialism and immaterialism are not logical contradictories and may both be
false.

I shall argue against materialism by setting up three
theses about thinking.

(I) *Thinking is an activity*. In Locke's phrase, we can be
'busy in thinking'. Thinking is something that can absorb
us, that we can throw ourselves into whole-heartedly, that
we can be distracted from or that can distract us from other
things, etc. All of these ways of describing an activity
fit thinking no less well than they fit physical activities like
billiards or football. In this respect the verb 'think' is widely

different from some other psychological verbs, e.g. the verbs 'mean' and 'understand', which do not relate to activities. Understanding is not an activity, because a claim on X's behalf that he understood can be justified only by X's having a certain capacity, and a capacity is not an activity. Again 'What were you doing all that time?' admits of the answer 'Thinking' but not the answer 'Understanding' ('Trying to understand' perhaps is a suitable answer—with an appropriate object understood for 'understand'—but to be engaged in trying to understand is to be thinking, not to be understanding). Again, a man's *bona fide* report is decisive as regards what he thought, but not as regards what he understood; a man may look as if he understood and claim *bona fide* to have understood and yet turn out not to have understood.

I may here interject a bit of theory. The doctrine of acts of understanding is quite wrongly attributed to the medieval scholastics. Though in ordinary Latin *'intelligere'* means 'understand', medieval Latin is often a standard rendering of Aristotle's Greek, and *'intelligere'* is Aristotle's *'noein'* which is Greek for 'to think of' not for 'to understand'. *'Homo actu intelligens lapidem'* in Aquinas's Latin thus means 'a man actually thinking of a stone', not 'understanding a stone' (whatever that is), nor even 'understanding the word "lapis"'. And *'actu intelligibile'* does not mean 'actually understandable', where the '-able' and the 'actually' seem to fight it out, with a doubtful issue; it renders *'energeiāi noēton'*, 'actually thought of', where *energeiāi*, 'actually', is needed to exclude the systematic ambiguity of these participles in *-ton* between being actually an object of ϕing and being ϕable. I suspect that a misconstruction of this medieval jargon may have led, historically, to the postulation of 'acts of understanding'.

Meaning something is in a rather different position; if a man professes *bona fide* to have just now meant something by what he said, then he did mean it, just as if he professes *bona fide* to have thought of something then he did think of it. And one can even tie meaning to a particular time—

'When he said — he meant —'. But there are other ways of telling that meaning something is not an act, not an episode in an activity. When the indignant father finds his house-guest teaching children to game with dice and says 'That's not the sort of game I meant!' he is not alluding to an act of meaning whereby he meant a different sort of game to be taught. And if someone tells you to start at 1 and go on writing down odd numbers in succession till told to stop, he can properly say he meant you to write 103 after 101, without himself having performed an act of meaning '103 after 101'. Nor can we be absorbed in, or distracted by or from, meaning things, as we can in regard to thinking.

This part of my paper is all taken from Wittgenstein, because I think he was right, and I'd sooner be right than original; also, because I think it may serve to correct a misunderstanding of what he was about. He is supposed to have had a long-term programme of eliminating all acts or activities of the mind, a programme that he thought he'd already pretty well completed as regards meaning and understanding; thinking, though, was a tougher problem. On the contrary: it is clear that he wanted to contrast psychological words that did relate to actual experiences and activities with those which did not; this was the whole point of such 'grammatical investigation' as I have been summarizing. And it brings out the point of saying that thinking *is* an activity if we contrast the verb 'think' with other psychological verbs that do not relate to activities.

I shall say little about the programme of reducing ostensibly categorical propositions about the activity of thinking to hypothetical propositions about what a man would overtly do in certain unrealized conditions. This is only a programme: no such analysis of any individual proposition has actually been given, and none, I think would be at all plausible. One may well wonder what the attraction of the programme is— especially when unfulfilled conditional statements are themselves so puzzling philosophically.

(II) *Thinking is a basic activity.* I speak of more basic and less basic activities in much the same way as Miss Anscombe spoke of more brute and less brute facts (in her *Analysis* paper 'On Brute Facts'). For example, in a given context C, action (1), inscribing certain marks on paper, is (2) writing a certain English sentence; and in a context C' (specified in more detail than C), writing the English sentence is (3) formulating a certain step in a philosophical argument. Again, in a given context C, action (1), uttering certain articulate noises, is (2) giving an order for goods to the grocer; and in the more closely specified context C', ordering from the grocer is (3) running further into debt. (Notice that in this case the context-of-action C' would be specified partly by negative conditions, e.g. that the man had no money to pay the debts he already had and no prospect of getting any.) In either example I say that action (1) is more basic than action (2), and action (2) than action (3); to do a less basic action always consists in doing a more basic action, a certain context of action being presupposed.

Now if action (1) is basic in relation to action (2), and action (1) is performed with an instrument N, it does not necessarily follow that we can speak likewise of performing (2) with N. Again, if action (1) can be ascribed to the instrument N as well as to the agent, it does not follow that action (2) can be so ascribed. For example, we can speak of writing an English sentence with a pen, we can even perhaps say that a pen writes an English sentence; but we can scarcely say that a step of an argument is formulated with a pen, and certainly we cannot say that a pen formulates a step of an argument. Again, if a man produces articulate sounds with his vocal organs, we may equally well say that his vocal organs produce articulate sounds; but we cannot say that his vocal organs order goods from the grocer, though we can perhaps say that he orders goods with his vocal organs; certainly we cannot say that a man runs further into debt with his vocal organs, as he runs away from his angry creditor with his legs, and still less can we say that his vocal organs ran him into debt.

One way, then, that the materialists might be wrong would be if thinking were not ascribable to any instrument because of its not being a basic activity. Discovery of such a mistake on the materialists' part need not, however, mean that our world-view need be very different from theirs. In any case, it seems to me that thinking is a basic activity; that there is not a more basic activity in which, given the context, the activity of thinking consists. If anyone holds otherwise, it is up to him to give an account of thinking as a non-basic activity. I know of no such account that is at all plausible. Perhaps someone might hold that in a given context to think certain thoughts is to have certain mental images, feelings, unspoken words, etc., passing through one's mind; but there are fairly obvious objections—in particular, that on many occasions of thinking thoughts, there seems to occur nothing of the sort that could be relevant.

(III) *The activity of thinking cannot be assigned a position in the physical time-series.* I shall approach this thesis by stages. First, I want to call your attention to the discontinuous character of thought—the complete inappropriateness of James's expression 'the stream of thought'. This is because each thought has a content which cannot pass over by a gradual transition to another content; if I have first the thought that lions are dangerous and then pass over to the thought that tigers are dangerous, this does not happen by a continuous change from the thought of a lion to the thought of a tiger. And even if a thought has a complex content, this does not mean that elements in this complex can occur separately or successively; the thought that all tigers are dangerous cannot consist in my first thinking of all tigers and then going on to think of danger. For, whatever B. F. Skinner may suppose, 'all tigers' is a phrase that has no meaning outside the context of a sentence, because 'all' is a word that does the job of showing how a predicate latches on to a subject; and similarly there is no such feat as thinking of all tigers except in the context of a thought that all tigers are so-and-so. Likewise, though I may no doubt have an indefinite thought of danger, a thought of tigers followed by such a thought would not be a thought that all tigers are dangerous; unless the whole content of the thought that all tigers are dangerous is simultaneously present to the thinker, no such thought occurs at all.

Thinking consists in having a series of thoughts which can be counted off discretely—the first, the second, the third, . . .—; which, if complex, must occur with all their elements present simultaneously; which do not pass into one another by gradual transition. The truth of the account is I think borne out by the vain attempts of William James, in the chapter of his *Principles* that I just alluded to, to establish the contrary. He attempts to show that in the thought (say) that the pack of cards is on the table there are successive phases, in which elements corresponding to the separate words of this *that* clause are severally and successively prominent; that even formal words like 'is' and 'if' and 'or' have meaning because they correspond to feelings of transition that are part of the stream of thought; that the content of a thought is not something expressible in language and communicable to others, but something that you can only recollect if you reproduce 'the thought as it was uttered, with every word fringed and the whole sentence bathed in that original halo of obscure relations'. It would take a long time to show all that is wrong in James's way of regarding the matter; I can now only say briefly that James's description of thought blurs out the logical features of thought, and makes it impossible to see why one cannot *think* nonsense though one can *talk* nonsense. (If you write down a nonsensical *that* clause after 'Smith has the thought . . . ', the whole sentence will be nonsense and thus cannot be a true report of what Smith thought; but there is no such difficulty about quoting the nonsense Smith talks.) Indeed, James expressly says that 'subjective sense' is a matter of a 'feeling of rational relation'. It is not surprising that later in his career James should have solemnly said 'I renounce logic'; I suppose it was in much the same spirit that Humphrey in his book on *Thinking* spoke of 'freeing psychology from the shackles of logic.'

If thoughts occur not in a Jamesian stream, but as I maintain that they do—as a series in which certain thought-contents successively occur, with no succession within any one thought and no gradual transition from one thought to another: then these thoughts, if they have position in the physical time-series, must occur either *legato* or *staccato*— either one thought's ending must immediately be the beginning of another thought, or there must a be time-gap of thoughtlessness in between thoughts. But are we in fact tied down to this alternative? Pains and other such sensory processes may be long or short, continuous or intermittent; but in spite of Longfellow's 'long, long thoughts', I do not think a thought (say, that the pack of cards is on the table, or that Geach's arguments are fallacious) can significantly be called long or short; nor are we obliged to say that in that case every thought must be strictly instantaneous.

The difficulty felt over saying that a thought need be neither long, nor short, nor instantaneous comes about, I suggest, from a (perhaps unacknowledged) assumption of a Newtonian or Kantian view of time: time is taken to be logically prior to events, events on the other hand must occupy divisible stretches or else indivisible instants of time. If we reject this view and think instead in terms of time-relations, then what I am suggesting is that thoughts have not got all the kinds of time-relations that physical events, and I think also sensory processes, have. One may say that during half an hour by the clock such-and-such a series of thoughts occurred to a man; but I think it is impossible to find a stretch of physical events that would be just simultaneous, or even simultaneous to a good approximation, with one of the thoughts in the series. I think Norman Malcolm was right when he said at a meeting in Oxford that a mental image could be before one's mind's eye for just as long as a beetle took to crawl across a table; but I think it would be nonsense to say that I 'was thinking' a given thought for the period of the beetle's crawl—the continuous past of 'think' has no such use. (The White Knight 'was thinking' of a plan in that he *thought* certain thoughts successively; and for each individual thought 'was thinking' would have no application.)

36

The feature of thinking for which I have just been arguing may well lead us to reconsider whether we ought to accept Thesis (II). For one way that we might readily explain why it is impossible to assign to individual acts of thinking a position in the physical time-scale is that thinking is not after all a basic activity. If a more basic activity is clockable, the same may not hold for a less basic activity performed in performing the more basic one. In a given context, which includes the subsequent drinking of the poison and the death of the victim, a man's laying poison for his wife is an act of murder; the laying of the poison is clockable, but when was the murder committed? When the poison was laid, or when it was drunk, or when the wife died? This is a matter for legal decision and it might be legally important, but philosophically speaking there is no right answer—the murder is not clockable. There is no mystery about this, no reason to say that murders occur in a non-physical time-scale; for murdering is not a basic activity, and the basic events involved—the laying of the poison, the drinking of the poison, the victim's illness and death—are all of them straightforwardly clockable. Similarly, if thinking were shown to be a less basic activity in relation to certain clock-able activities, we might perhaps cease to be puzzled by the fact that some questions about the time-relations of thinking to physical events are in principle unanswerable. This, I think, is the point at which my argument should be most closely scrutinized. But so far as I can see, thinking *is* a basic activity.

If thinking is a basic activity, the truth of Thesis (III) entails that materialism is false—that thinking is not the activity of the brain or of any bodily organ. For the basic activities of any bodily part must be clockable in physical time in a way that thinking is not. No physiological discoveries could establish that thoughts occurred precisely when certain brain-processes occurred; and *a fortiori* the suggestion that the brain-processes might be identical with the thoughts does not even deserve discussion.

Materialism, then, is false: but it does not follow that

immaterialism is true. You will remember that for present purposes immaterialism is the doctrine that a man thinks with an immaterial part of himself, his mind or soul. There is no direct way of inferring this from the falsity of materialism. If a man does not think with a material part of himself, we cannot infer that he does think with an immaterial part of himself; unless we first assume that in any event a man thinks with some part of himself, which may be material or immaterial. Indeed, it is difficult to make sense of the expression 'immaterial part', even if you say 'constituent' instead of 'part'.

It is a savage superstition to suppose that a man consists of two pieces, body and soul, which come apart at death; the superstition is not mended but rather aggravated by conceptual confusion, if the soul-piece is supposed to be immaterial. The genius of Plato and Descartes has given this superstition an undeservedly long lease of life; it gained some accidental support from Scriptual language, e.g. about flesh and spirit—accidental, because a Platonic-Cartesian reading of such passages is mistaken, as Scripture scholars now generally agree. In truth, a man *is* a sort of body, not a body *plus* an immaterial somewhat; for a man is an animal, and an animal is one kind of living body; and thinking is a vital activity of a man, not of any part of him, material or immaterial. The only tenable conception of the soul is the Aristotelian conception of the soul as the form, or actual organization, of the living body; and thus you may say a man thinks with his soul, if you mean positively that thinking is a vital activity, an activity of a living being, and negatively that thinking is not performed by any bodily organ.

In our present experience we encounter thought as an activity of organisms. But since thought is in principle not locatable in the physical time-continuum, as the vegetative, and I think also the sensitive, activities or organisms are, there is a logically open possibility that thought should occur independently, not as the activity of a living organism. We can even conceive, I think, of there being evidence that this possibility were realized. For thought, which is only contingently connected with the physiological processes in a human body, is more than contingently connected with the characteristic works and expressions of thought: in particular with language. The non-contingent connexion of thought with language, the intrinsic intelligibility of language structure, is shown in the fact—rightly emphasized by Wittgenstein, often ignored by psychologists—that we can express new thoughts with old words and can understand an impromptu; nothing could be more inept than to call the speaking or understanding of language a matter of 'learned reactions'. It is this intrinsic intelligibility of language that makes translation machines work. The origination of the logical structure embodied in language is not just evidence of thinking; it *is* thinking, and its relation to language is one of formal, not efficient, causality. (I do not say this is the only sort of thinking.)

This much premised, let us imagine that over a period of time a roulette wheel gives only the numbers 1 to 26, and that this sequence of numbers spells out English sentences according to the obvious code (A = 1, B = 2, etc.) Let us further imagine that this goes on although the most elaborate precautions are taken against physical tampering with the wheel. All of this is clearly possible and raises no conceptual difficulties. I submit that we could then have conclusive evidence that the thoughts normally expressible by the English sentences in question were being originated, and strong evidence that they were originated by no living organism. The question how the thoughts could be supposed to 'influence' the roulette wheel appears to me a spurious one; I have already sufficiently described how the thoughts would be embodied in the numbers spelt out by the wheel; and it is just a mistake to suppose that we need to add a story about para-mechanical transference of para-energy, or that such an addition would be intelligible.

This and the like examples can show the possibility of disembodied thought; thought unconnected with any living organism. And some continuing disembodied thought might have such connexion with the thoughts I have as a living man as to constitute my survival as a 'separated soul'. To be sure, such survival must sound a meagre and unsatisfying thing; particularly if it is the case, as I should hold, that there is no question of sensations and warm human feelings and mental images existing apart from a living organism. But I do not want the prospect to be anything but bleak; I am of the mind of Aquinas about the survival of 'separated souls', when he says in his commentary on I Corinthians that my soul is not I, and if only my soul is saved then I am not saved nor is any man. Even if Christians believe there are 'separate souls', the Christian hope is the glorious resurrection of the body, not the survival of a 'separated soul'.

I have said nothing so far about the ascription of thinking to machines. On this matter I shall be quite brief. Machines manifestly have no life, no sense, no feelings, no purposes except their makers'; there is just no question of ascribing to them the activity of thinking. I may be challenged, e.g. to define life, since I say machines have no life. But I am not logically bound to notice this challenge; to think I am bound to is simply an old fallacy—we might well call it Socrates' fallacy—which infers lack of knowledge whether a given thing is X or not from inability to produce a criterion for Xness that will work even in the odd or marginal case. And we just do know machines are not alive, even as we know Queen Anne is no longer alive; the case is not odd or marginal.

I have argued that thinking is an activity that cannot possibly be performed by any organic part of a living being. But even if this were possible, it would leave thinking as a vital activity, which can only be performed by a living being. And whereas a man can walk with an artificial leg, it would be an absurd fantasy to imagine his going on thinking with an artificial *Denkapparat* which was substituted for a damaged brain. Even if a brain thinks, a prosthetic 'brain' would not.

The arguments used to the contrary are often frivolously bad. For example: that machines sometimes surprise their makers, so presumably they have minds of their own. Or:

that we need not bother about machines being inorganic, because this objection to regarding them as alive could be got over by using wooden or plastic parts. Or: that a machine manifests something like vanity behaviour when, being constructed to seek light sources, it oscillates to and fro in front of a mirror (because of the mirror's virtual image). Such arguments give an impression of willing self-deception. And it is really sinister when those who then deceive themselves envisage a future where man will have constructed machines which not only really think but think much more wisely than we, and can be profitably consulted on such important matters as how many babies to allow to be born and when to start massacring our enemies. It is a suitable Nemesis of human pride that men should thus be getting ready to perform acts of brutish idolatry—to humble themselves before the superior minds that they, like the heathen before them, believe they can get to inhabit inanimate artefacts.

4

Form and Existence

In this paper I shall discuss what Aquinas meant by his term *esse*, or *actus essendi*, 'act of existing'. Another synonym that he uses—*quo aliquid est*, 'that by which a thing is (or: exists)'—suggests a convenient division of the subject: we can first discuss Aquinas's philosophical use of *quo*, 'that by which', and then consider which sense of *est*, which sort of existential proposition, may be relevant to Aquinas's doctrine of *esse*. But we shall see that, having got thus far, we cannot arrive at the meaning of the whole phrase, *quo aliquid est*, or the reasons for the way Aquinas uses it, simply by combining our separate considerations about *quo* and *est*.

I

Beginning with Aquinas's use of *quo* brings a great immediate advantage. The predicate *est*, 'is' or 'exists', is at least a peculiar one, and many people would deny that it is properly a predicate at all; but Aquinas uses *quo* not only with *est* but also with unexceptionable predicates. In this use, *quo* followed by a noun subject and an (ordinary) predicate is synonymous with the phrase formed by the abstract noun answering to the predicate followed by the genitive of the noun that was subject; *quo Socrates albus est* ('that by which Socrates is white') is synonymous with *albedo Socratis* ('the whiteness of Socrates') and so on. Either kind of phrase is thus used in order to designate what Aquinas calls Forms; to understand his use of *quo* we must examine his notion of

42

forms, which moreover is intimately connected in other ways with his doctrine of *esse*.

For Aquinas, the real distinction between a form and the self-subsistent individual (*suppositum*) whose form it is comes out in the logical distinction between subject and predicate (Ia q.13 art.12; q.85 art.5 ad 3 um). I think this is the way to introduce his notion of form to modern philosophers. There are, however, strong prejudices against allowing that this logical distinction answers to *any* real distinction. One such obstacle is the old two-name or identity theory of predication, which flourished in the Middle Ages, and still keeps on appearing in new guises: the theory that a true predication is effected by joining different names of the same thing or things, the copula being a sign of this real identity. I shall not waste time on this logically worthless theory. Anybody who is tempted by it may try his hand at explaining in terms of it how we can fit together the three terms 'David', 'father', and 'Solomon' (which on this theory are three *names*) to form the true predication 'David is the father of Solomon'.

The futility of the two-name theory comes out clearly at the beginning of Lewis Carroll's *Game of Logic*. Lewis Carroll professes to find a difficulty over saying 'some pigs are pink'; as it stands, this suggests an impossible identity between certain things (pigs) and a certain attribute (signified by 'pink')! He seeks to remove this difficulty by expounding the proposition as meaning 'some pigs are pink pigs', where 'are' signifies real identity. But 'pink pigs' means 'pigs that are pink', and there is as much or as little difficulty about this phrase as about the predication 'pigs are pink' at which he stumbles.

If noun-phrases like 'thing that runs' can properly be regarded as names (a difficult problem of logical theory that cannot be discussed here), then it *is* possible to state the truth-condition of an affirmative predication as an identity of reference between two names; 'a man runs', let us say, is true if and only if 'man' and 'thing that runs' are two names of the same individual. Aquinas uses this way of stating

43

truth-conditions quite often, and has in consequence been wrongly regarded as holding the two-name theory. But it is not the name 'thing that runs' that is used in the sentence 'a man runs', but the predicate 'runs' from which this name is formed; and 'runs' and 'thing that runs' are by no means synonymous; the relation between their ways of signifying in fact raises over again the same problem as the relation of subject and predicate, a problem that is thus merely shifted by expressing the truth-conditions of predication in terms of identity of reference.

Modern philosophers have pretty generally abandoned the two-name theory; at least to the extent of admitting that a logical subject and a predicate have radically different ways of signifying. But need we admit also a difference of type as regards the realities signified? Surely what distinguishes a predicate from a name is just the fact that it does not *name* anything, but is rather true or false *of* things; a true predication is one in which the predicate *is true of* what the subject *names*. Are we not blurring this distinction if we say that predicates stand for (why not, that they *name?*) a type of entity other than that which names stand for? Have not philosophers said the queerest things about the entities that predicates are supposed to stand for? No wonder; such paradoxes are bound to arise if you treat as a name what is not a name; like the paradoxes about Nobody in *Through the Looking-glass*.

But, whatever difficulties it may involve, I think we have to allow that logical predicates do stand for something, as well as being true or false *of* things. For when a question *how many* is asked and answered, we can surely ask: To what is this manyness being ascribed? And in any concrete instance we shall find that in asserting manyness we use a logically predicative word or phrase, and are ascribing manyness to what this stands for. 'How many ducks are swimming in the Chamberlain Fountain?' 'Three.' If this answer were true, there would be objects of which 'duck swimming in the Chamberlain Fountain' could truly be predicated; and my number-statement is about what this predicate stands for. You cannot say my statement ascribes a property (threeness) to a certain set of individuals—the ducks swimming in the Chamberlain Fountain. So far as I know no ducks *are* swimming there; and it makes no difference whether there are any or not; for the sense of the question how many such ducks there are cannot depend on what the right answer to the question is. Now the answer 'three' cannot be taken as a predication about a set of ducks unless the question answered is a question about them; but the question how many such ducks there are *admits* of the answer 'o'; and noughtishness certainly is not here being taken as a property of any set of ducks. You may indeed rightly say that my proposition is about *ducks* (not: *the* ducks) swimming in the Chamberlain Fountain. The omission of the definite article is here significant. A proposition that could rightly be called 'a proposition about *the* ducks (etc.)' would have to refer (or at least profess to refer) to a certain set of ducks; but in speaking of 'a proposition about ducks (etc.)' I am not implying that the proposition mentions any individual ducks, but on the contrary that it is about what the predicate 'duck swimming in the Chamberlain Fountain' stands for.

It is only to what such a predicative expression stands for that we can even falsely ascribe manyness. It is nonsense, unintelligible, not just false, to ascribe manyness to an individual; what can be repeated is always and only a common nature. *Non enim potest in intellectum cadere pluralitas huius individui* (Ia. q.13 art.9). Because, for Aquinas, forms are what answer *in rebus* to logical predicates, it is consistent for him to say that forms are as such multipliable (Ia. q.3 art.2 ad 3 um: q.7 art.1).

I cannot help being reminded here of the very similar language that we find in Frege. Frege, like Aquinas, held that there was a fundamental distinction *in rebus* answering to the logical distinction between subject and predicate— the distinction between *Gegenstand* (object) and *Begriff* (concept). (In using *Begriff* as a term for what logical predicates represent, Frege was not accepting any form of conceptualism; on the contrary, he explicitly denies that the *Begriff* is any creature of the human mind—it is, he says, 'objective'.) And for Frege the *Begriff*, and it alone, admits of repetition and manyness; an object cannot be repeated—*kommt nie widerholt vor.*

Understood in this way, the distinction between individual and form is absolutely sharp and rigid; what can sensibly be said of one becomes nonsense if we try to say it of the other. (Aquinas's 'subsistent forms' might seem to bridge the gulf; but, as we shall presently see, they do not, nor did Aquinas really think they do.) Just because of this sharp distinction, we must reject the Platonic doctrine that what a predicate stands for is some single entity over against its many instances, *hen epi pollôn.* On the contrary: the common nature that the predicate 'man' (say) stands for can be indifferently one or many, and neither oneness nor manyness is a mark or note of human nature itself. This point is very clearly made by Aquinas in *De Ente et Essentia.* Again we find Frege echoing Aquinas; Frege counts oneness or manyness (as the case may be) among the properties (*Eigenschaften*) of a concept, which means that it cannot at the same time be one of the marks or notes (*Merkmalen*) of that concept. (Frege's choice of words is here unfortunate; his saying that it is an *Eigenschaft*, e.g. of human nature to be found in many individuals has led people to suppose that he regards this as a *proprium* of human nature—although so to read him makes complete nonsense of his distinction. Aquinas's saying that oneness or manyness is incidental, *accidit*, to human nature is a much clearer expression.)

The Platonic mistake about the nature of forms goes with a liberal use of what we may class together as abstract-singular expressions like 'X-ness' or 'the attribute of being X'; these expressions are not just grammatically but also logically, argumentatively, handled as though they were proper names. I do not say that such abstract expressions looking like proper names should be totally banned; it would make things very difficult for philosophers. (I myself used 'human nature' in this way in the last paragraph.) But

I do say that anyone who uses them ought to be ready to replace them on demand by use of the concrete predicates from which they are derived. (Thus: for 'neither oneness nor manyness is a mark of human nature itself' read 'whether there is one man or many men is irrelevant to what X must be if X is a man', or something like that.) Sometimes this replacement is stylistically better, sometimes not. But it must be possible; a sentence with an *irreducible* abstract 'proper name' in it (say: 'Redness is an eternal object') is nonsense.

All the same, Platonism of this sort is a very great temptation; and I think it is instructive to watch Frege's unsuccessful struggles against temptation in his paper *Ueber Begriff und Gegenstand* ('On Concept and Object'). I quote (op. cit., p. 197):

> In logical discussions one quite often needs to assert something about a concept, and to express this in the form usual for such assertions, viz. to make what is asserted of the concept into the content of the grammatical predicate. Consequently, one would expect that the reference of the grammatical subject would be the concept; but the concept as such cannot play this part, in view of its predicative nature; it must first be converted into an object, or, speaking more precisely, represented by an object. We designate this object by prefixing the words 'the concept': e.g.
>
> 'The concept *man* is not empty'.
>
> Here the first three words are to be regarded as a proper name.

And later on (p. 198): 'In my way of speaking, expressions like "the concept F" designate not concepts but objects.'

Of course Frege has gone astray here: he does not clear himself of the charge of having made a concept into an object just by saying that 'the concept *man*' does not stand for a concept but for an object that 'represents' a concept; no more than a writer can escape the charge of vulgarity by a parenthetical 'to use a vulgarism'. But how then are we to get into the subject of predication a direct reference to what Frege calls a concept and Aquinas calls a form? I think the solution, the way to avoid the mistake of Platonism, is that an abstract noun (or noun-phrase) referring to the form can indeed occupy the place of the subject, but cannot be the whole of the subject; the form being signified, *in recto* as Aquinas would say, by an abstract noun, we must add a mention *in obliquo* of the individual whose form it is; 'the wisdom of Socrates' and 'the redness of Socrates's nose' give us designations of forms, the spurious proper names 'wisdom' and 'redness' do not.

We must not construe 'the wisdom of Socrates' as 'wisdom which Socrates possesses': apart from lapsing into the Platonic error of taking 'wisdom' as a singular term, we should run into notorious antinomies about the relation supposedly meant by 'possesses'. 'Of' in 'the wisdom of Socrates' does not signify a special relation, as in such phrases as 'the statue of Socrates' or 'the shield of Socrates'. The statue is *of* Socrates by being related to him in one way, the shield is *of* Socrates by being related to him in another way; but if we start saying 'and the wisdom is *of* Socrates . . .' we have already gone wrong, for logically 'the wisdom of Socrates' does not split up into 'the wisdom' and 'of Socrates' (sc. 'that wisdom which is *of* Socrates') but into 'the wisdom of . . .' and 'Socrates'. What refers to a form is 'the wisdom of . . .', not the whole phrase 'the wisdom of Socrates'; 'the wisdom of . . .' needs to be completed with a name of something that has the form, just as the predicate '. . . is wise', which also stands for this form, needs to be completed by a subject.

'Of' is a logically inseparable part of the sign 'the wisdom of . . .', indicating the need to put a name after this sign; and this need is what makes the sign suitable to express a form, since a form, as Aquinas says, is more properly termed *entis* than *ens* (Ia. q.45 art.4). The linguistic oddity of the division into 'the wisdom of . . .' and 'Socrates'— a division that cannot be made in Latin at all—is quite trivial and accidental; in Hebrew, for example, such a division would be perfectly natural, since 'the wisdom of Socrates' would be rendered by inflecting the word for 'wisdom' and leaving the name 'Socrates' uninflected.

It may be asked: How *can* a form be designated both by a logical predicate like '. . . is wise' *and* by an expression like 'the wisdom of . . .'? These sorts of expressions are certainly not interchangeable; but I think we can show that the difference between them is only *secundum modum significandi*, not *secundum rem significatam;* it relates to the way we are talking about a form, and makes no difference to which form we are talking about. When we want to mention a form for the sake of expressing the supposition that in a given individual that form is found, we refer to it by an expression which together with the name of that individual forms a proposition—i.e., by a logical predicate like 'is wise'. But when we want to talk directly about the form itself, to get a reference to the form into the subject-place in our proposition, then we need to refer to the form by an expression which, together with a reference *in obliquo* to that in which the form is found, will compose a complex that can replace a logical subject—e.g. the expression 'the wisdom of . . .'.

It admittedly looks queer that a form cannot be designated either (say) by 'redness' alone or by 'the redness of Socrates's nose', but only by 'the redness of . . .' (understood to be followed by some name or other). We may help our understanding by the analogous case of functions in mathematics: neither the isolated square-root sign nor (say) '$\sqrt{25}$' designates a function, but rather the circumstance that the square-root sign is followed by some numeral or other.

This comparison of forms to functions in mathematics seems to me very useful; it was suggested to me by Frege's assimilation of his *Begriffe* to mathematical functions. (Frege indeed held that *Begriffe are* a sort of functions, which can take only two values, the 'true' value and the 'false' value; I shall not try to explain here this part of his doctrine, and would emphasize that I am asserting no more than an analogy between forms and functions.) It may for instance help us to see how 'of' in 'the wisdom of Socrates' does not stand for a special relation of 'inherence in' or 'belonging to'. Somebody ignorant of mathematics might take 'the square root of 25' to mean 'that one among square

49

roots which belongs to 25', and wonder how one number can 'belong' to another; but somebody who understands the term 'square root' can already understand 'square root of 25' and can see that a relation of 'belonging' does not come in. So also somebody who understands the term 'wisdom', and does not Platonically misunderstand it as a proper name, already understands the make-up of the phrase 'wisdom of Socrates' without needing to understand the mythical relation of inherence. The term 'wisdom', like the term 'square root', of itself demands a genitive to complete its sense.

Again, in the sense of the word 'form' that we have so far used, what the phrase 'the wisdom of Socrates' designates is not a form *simpliciter*; but can legitimately be said to be a form *of* Socrates, a form occurring in Socrates. This too can be elucidated by our mathematical analogy. Consider the square-root function: we cannot say that the number 5 is that function or any other function, but we can say that the number 5 is that function *of* the number 25. So also the wisdom of Socrates is not a form *simpliciter* but *is* a form *of* or *in* Socrates. What designates a form is not the whole phrase 'the wisdom of Socrates', but merely 'the wisdom of . . .'—although without completion this latter phrase is senseless.

Now at this point I think Aquinas's terminology is defective. He emphatically rejects the Platonic error of taking 'wisdom' as the proper name of a form; he says, e.g. that when (pseudo-) Dionysius speaks of life *per se* and wisdom *per se*, we are not to take this authority to be meaning certain self-subsistent entities (*quasdam subsistentes res*) (Ia. q.44 art.3 ad 4 um). But he often uses the term 'form' for what is referred to by a phrase like '*sapientia Socratis*' (the wisdom of Socrates'); whereas if we keep to the sense of 'form' that we have so far used, a sense that is also to be found in Aquinas, what designates a form is rather '*sapientia*' together with the genitive inflexion of the following noun. The syntax of Latin impedes clear statement of this point, and Aquinas could not, of course, use our mathematical analogy for elucidation.

I am here leaving myself open to the charge of developing

a new doctrine of form and departing from Aquinas's own doctrine. But if we will not impute to Aquinas a slight and natural inexactness of language at this point, then his doctrine of form becomes mere inconsistency and nonsense. For 'the wisdom of *Socrates*' must designate something individual, something that is no more multipliable or expressible by a predicate than Socrates himself is; so if this is taken to be a typical designation of a form, the whole distinction between form and individual is undone. To keep our heads clear, we must distinguish two senses of 'form' in Aquinas—the form that is the reference of the predicate '. . . is wise' or of the phrase 'the wisdom of . . .', and the form that is the reference of a phrase like 'the wisdom of Socrates'. In the latter case I shall speak of individualized forms; individualized forms will then not be forms *simpliciter* (just as a number that is a certain function of another number is not a function *simpliciter*) and will always be referred to by the full style 'individualized forms'.

This distinction is needed in order to make Aquinas's doctrine of subsistent or separate forms logically intelligible. When Aquinas tells us that God is wisdom itself, *Deus est ipsa sapientia*, he is not meaning that God is that of which the noun 'wisdom' is a proper name; for the Platonists are wrong in thinking that there is such an object, and Aquinas says that they are wrong. But we *can* take it to mean that 'God' and 'the wisdom of God' both designate the same thing; and this interpretation does not make Aquinas guilty of the impossible and nonsensical attempt to bridge the distinction previously expounded between form and individual, or find something intermediate. For we can significantly say that 'God' and 'the wisdom of God' and 'the power of God' are three terms with the same reference; but 'the wisdom of . . .' and 'the power of . . .' have not the same reference, any more than the predicates 'wise' and 'powerful' have. *Non dicimus quod attributum potentiae sit attributum scientiae, licet dicamus quod scientia (Dei) sit potentia (Dei)* (Ia. q.32 art. 3 ad 3 um).

This account, it may be argued, departs fatally from

Aquinas's mind, in that it makes out that in 'the wisdom of God' and 'the power of God', 'the wisdom of' and 'the power of' differ in reference from the word 'God' and from one another; for this conflicts with Aquinas's teaching on the divine simplicity. But what *we* signify by 'the wisdom of' and 'the power of' is really distinct; otherwise 'the wisdom of Socrates' would coincide in reference with 'the power of Socrates'. On the other hand what we signify by 'the wisdom of' is not, and is not signified as being, a part or element of what we signify by 'the wisdom of God', i.e. (according to Aquinas) God himself. If one designation is part of another, it does not follow that the things designated are respectively part and whole. 'The square root of 25' is a complex designation having as parts the designations 'the square root of' and '25'; but it does not follow (as Frege oddly inferred) that there is some sense of 'part' in which we may suitably say that the number 5, which is the square root of 25, has two heterogeneous parts—the square-root function and the number 25. Again—to get an analogy to the three designations 'God', 'the wisdom of God', 'the power of God'—the square and the cube are quite distinct functions, but '1' and 'the square of 1' and 'the cube of 1' all designate the same number, and there is no distinction even in thought between the 1 that is the square and the 1 that is the cube and the 1 that is squared and cubed.

The supposition that x itself is that by (or in virtue of) which x is F is certainly not logically absurd on the face of it (as would be the supposition that x was identical with the reference of the predicate 'F', an individual with a form). It will be instructive to consider an example from modern philosophy in which the assertion of identity between x and what makes x to be F might seem plausible, and to see why such identity must be here denied. The red-patch school of philosophy might well wish to say that a red patch in a sense-field neither is the red-patchiness of some other individual (of a *suppositum*) nor yet has any individualized forms distinct from itself. That in virtue of which the patch is red, that in virtue of which it is *so* big, that in virtue of which it is square, is nothing other than the patch itself, which is red, *so* big, and square.

But now let us observe our red square; after a short time it begins a gradual change, and the outer region of the square becomes green, while an inner region remains red and is circular in shape. Are we then to say 'The red was square and larger, and has become circular and smaller', or rather 'The square was all red and has become partly green'? Plainly we may say either—or rather *both*. But now the individual red and the individual square appear as distinct individual things, each with its own distinct persisting identity; there is no third individual, the red square; *rubrum et quadratum non est ens*. I do not mean, of course, that there cannot be a red square *object*; but then the persistent identity of this object will not consist in any simple sensible character like redness or squareness. It is because the philosophers' red square is supposed to have no characteristics except a few simple sensible ones that it falls to pieces under examination; for to each such character there answers a distinct individual reality, an individualized form—an individual extension, colour, shape, etc.—and though these are united in one *suppositum x* as the redness of *x*, the squareness of *x*, etc., they are not all one thing, the red patch; the red patch has no identity of its own, *non est vere unum nec vere ens*.

These examples of individualized forms may be objectionable to some people as factitious philosophical examples. But a wave, for example, is an identifiable individual that can move locally (although Professor Prichard *knew* that it was nonsense to say so); and this is certainly an individualized form—it is that by which a certain body of water is in a certain shape over part of its surface.

II

The expression 'that by which the individual *x* is (or: exists)' is senseless unless there is a sense in which 'is' or 'exists' is properly predicable of individuals. Now many modern philosophers would deny that there is such a sense:

'exists' is not a predicate. This maxim is often glibly and thoughtlessly used, but it has a serious use; it is an attempt to resolve the paradox of reference that arises over the denial of existence. For we *can* significantly and truly deny existence; indeed I should hold that there is no sense of 'exists' for which we do not get significant and true denials of existence. (Some philosophers have thought otherwise—that for a certain sense of the verb 'to be' 'A is' or 'A's are' is a form of proposition that is always true; even dragons *are*, even round squares *are*, in this sense! But at any rate to a discussion of Aquinas this supposed sense is irrelevant; we may stick to the everyday senses of 'to be' or 'to exist' for which existence *can* be truly denied.) How is such denial possible? It might look as though 'A is not' or 'A does not exist' were never true; for if it were, the subject-term 'A' would fail to have reference, and so no predication would have been made at all, let alone a true predication.

We can get out of this difficulty by denying that in 'A is not' or 'A does not exist' the verb 'is' or 'exists' is a logical predicate. For since 'subject' and 'predicate' are correlatives, this is tantamount to denying that the grammatical subject 'A' is a logical subject. And from this again it follows that the proposition 'A does not exist' is not really about what the subject 'A' ostensibly stands for; so in asserting the proposition we do not fall into the absurdity of using 'A' as though it stood for something and then in effect denying that it does so.

But though saying that 'exists' or 'is' is not a genuine logical predicate of individuals would thus resolve the paradox of non-existence, this does not prove that it is not, sometimes at least, a genuine logical predicate; for the paradox might be resoluble some other way. Moreover, it is not enough to say that in 'A does not exist' 'A' cannot be the genuine subject of predication, unless at the same time we can bring out the real logical role of 'A'—the real logical nature of existential propositions.

I think it is a great mistake to treat all existential propositions as having the same logical status. I am not here concerned with the familiar thesis that existence is an analogical notion—that questions of existence are different according to what it is whose existence is in question, a God, an historical character, an animal species, a sub-atomic particle . . . Quite apart from these differences, we have to recognize three different kinds of existential proposition even about the same kind of things—e.g. about the existence of living creatures. The difference perhaps comes out best when we take negative propositions as our examples.

A. There is no such thing as Cerberus; Cerberus does not exist, is not real.
B. There is no such thing as a dragon; dragons do not exist.
C. Joseph is not and Simeon is not.

The A proposition that I gave as an example might typically be used to comfort a child who had been frightened by hearing Greek myths and thought Cerberus would come and bite him. 'Cerberus', we might say 'doesn't exist (is not real) like Rover'. Here we are not pointing out any trait that Cerberus has and Rover lacks; for it would be nonsense to speak of the trait of *being what there is such a thing as*, and more nonsense to say that some things (e.g. Rover) have this trait, while other things (e.g. Cerberus) lack it, and are thus things that there is no such thing as. Logically our proposition is about a difference not between two dogs, Cerberus and Rover, but between the uses of two words 'Cerberus' and 'Rover'. The word 'Rover' is seriously used to refer to something and does in fact so refer; the word 'Cerberus' is a term that we only make believe has reference.

Since 'Cerberus does not exist' and 'Rover does exist' have not (as they seem to have) the names of two dogs as their logical subjects—since we are not here *using* 'Cerberus' and 'Rover' as names, but talking *about* their use—it is appropriate to say that in A propositions 'exists' or 'is real' is not a predicate, not even of the word 'Cerberus'. To show the real force of the parent's reassuring 'Cerberus does not exist', and how it is about the word 'Cerberus', we cannot content ourselves with writing '(The word) "Cerberus" does not exist', but must completely recast the sentence, say as follows: 'When I said "Cerberus" in that story, I was only pretending to use it as a name'.

As regards the B proposition 'there is no such thing as a dragon' or 'dragons do not exist', it is equally clear that this cannot be referring to an attribute of *being what there is such a thing as*, which cows have and dragons lack. But there is also a great difference between A and B propositions. In the A proposition we have an ostensible use of a proper name; in the B proposition we have a descriptive, predicable expression like 'cow' or 'dragon'—what Frege would have called a *Begriffswort* (concept-word).

The difference between A and B propositions may perhaps come out better if I shift to another pair of examples. A certain astronomer claimed to have identified an intra-Mercurian planet, which he christened 'Vulcan'. His claim was not substantiated; and a modern astronomer would accordingly say 'Vulcan did not exist' (an A proposition); he would also say 'So far as we know, an intra-Mercurian planet does not exist' (a B proposition). The force of the A proposition is to deprecate the premature introduction of the term 'Vulcan' into astronomical discourse. But in the B proposition the astronomer does not deprecate the use of the term 'intra-Mercurian planet', but himself uses that term to make a scientific remark. He is not, however, using the term as a name, as a subject of predication, but as a logical predicate. 'There is no intra-Mercurian planet' means 'nothing at all is an intra-Mercurian planet'. (Similarly, the affirmative B proposition 'there is a hairless cat' means 'something or other is a hairless cat'.) Now the use of a logical predicate in general does not commit you to allowing that there is something it applies to; it does so commit you if you make an affirmative assertion with that as the predicate but not if e.g. you use the predicate negatively or in the antecedent or consequent of a hypothetical. So saying 'nothing whatever is an intra-Mercurian planet' does not commit you to allowing that there is after all such a planet.

The importance of B propositions is that the question

whether there is *a* so-and-so, what Aquinas calls the question *an est?*, has to be answered with an affirmative or negative B proposition. Aquinas realized the logical peculiarity of B propositions: that the B proposition 'an F exists' does not attribute actuality to an F, but F-ness to something or other; e.g. 'there is evil' does not mean 'evil has actual existence' but 'some things have defects' (Ia. q.48 art.2 ad 2 um). And let us not think this is so because of some peculiarity of the term 'evil'; Aquinas speaks of the question *an est?* quite generally in the place I have cited, and says that the 'existence' involved in a true affirmative answer to it consists in the truth of an affirmative predication (*compositio*). This is exactly right, for 'an F exists' is true if and only if 'F' is truly predicable of something or other. Moreover, the same logical status is expressly ascribed to 'God exists', or 'there is a God' (Ia. q.3 art.4 ad 2 um); and Aquinas expressly denies that this proposition relates to what *he* calls God's *esse* or *actus essendi*. (This most important negative indication as to how we must understand the term *esse* has often been overlooked.) In 'God exists' we are not predicating something of God, but predicating the term 'God' itself; 'God exists' means 'something or other is God'. When we see this, we can steer our way safely through all the shoals of the seventeenth-century ontological argument. (Though it is commonly called by the same name, I think Anselm's argument is essentially different; I shall not here discuss it.)

It is important that for Aquinas 'God' is a descriptive, predicable, term (*nomen naturae*—Frege's *Begriffswort*) and not a logically proper name. Only because of this can the question whether there is one God or many make sense; just as the question whether there is one sun or many makes sense only if 'sun' is used to mean 'heavenly body of such-and-such a nature', not if it is a proper name of *this* heavenly body (Ia. q. 13 art.9). Only because of this can the heathen say his idol is God and the Christian contradict him and both be using 'God' in the same sense; if 'God' were a proper name, it would be a logically impossible, not a lying, wicked, act, to predicate it of sticks and stones (Ia. q.13 art.10).

This may seem to raise difficulties about another view of Aquinas I have discussed—that 'God' in the context of the phrases 'the power of God' and 'the wisdom of God' has the same reference with either of these phrases, namely God himself. If 'God' is a predicative expression, how can it significantly stand in place of a proper name like 'Socrates', after 'the wisdom of' or 'the power of'? I think it is enough to reply that 'God' in *such* contexts, or indeed in subject position before 'is wise' or 'is powerful', has the force of a definite description—'the one and only God'; whatever our theory of descriptions may be, it will have to yield the result that a definite description can significantly take the place of a proper name, as subject of a proposition or again after a phrase like 'the wisdom of'.

We now come on to C propositions like 'Joseph is not and Simeon is not'. It would be quite absurd to say that Jacob in uttering these words was not talking about Joseph and Simeon but about the use of their names. Of course he was talking about his sons; he was expressing a fear that something had happened to them, that they were dead. We have here a sense of 'is' or 'exists' that seems to me to be certainly a genuine predicate of individuals; the sense of 'exist' in which one says that an individual came to exist, still exists, no longer exists, etc.; the sense of 'to be' in which God says of himself 'I am who *am*' (i.e. 'I am he who *is*'), or in which Homer spoke of the Gods who ever are, *aien eontes*. Now why should one suspect that this cannot be a genuine predicate of individuals? The fact that in A and B propositions the verb 'exist' or 'be' is not such a genuine predicate tells us nothing about C propositions.

Moreover, we cannot argue that if the C proposition 'x is not' is true, then the subject term 'x' no longer has anything to refer to and therefore no predication has been made. As Wittgenstein says (*Philosophische Untersuchungen* I.§40): 'That is to confound the reference (*Bedeutung*) of the name with the bearer of the name. When Mr. N. N. dies, we say that the bearer of the name dies, not that the reference dies. And it would be nonsensical to say that; for if the named ceased to have reference, it would make nonsense to say "Mr. N.N. is dead" '. To put the same thing another way: The reference of a name admits of no time qualifications names are tenseless. Octavian was not known as 'Augustus' till quite later in his career; but once the name was in established use with that reference, it could be used by anybody at any time, in relation to any stage of Octavian's career (e.g. in answering the question 'Where was Augustus born?') and regardless of whether Octavian was alive or dead. So negative C propositions can raise no paradoxes of reference—and in showing this we had no need to deny that in them 'is' or 'exists' is a genuine predicate.

Now it is *this* sense of 'is' or 'exists', the one found in C propositions, that is relevant to Aquinas's term *esse*. This interpretation, I maintain, alone makes coherent sense of all that Aquinas says about *esse*.

It is worth noticing that as regards living beings 'to be' (in the C sense) has the same reference as 'to live', *vivere viventibus est esse* (Ia. q.18 art.2). This may confirm us against sophistical attempts to show that the verb 'to be' in this sense is not a genuine predicate of individuals. 'Poor Fred was alive and is dead'; how could one argue that this is not a genuine predication about poor Fred? and what difference does it make if we say instead 'poor Fred *was*, and *is not*'?

Some people may not easily see the difference between 'God exists' (sense B) and 'God is' (sense C). But in the contradictories the difference is apparent. 'God is not' (sense C) would have to be construed like 'Joseph is not'; it would then suitably express the supposition that perhaps the world was made by an old superannuated God who has since died (a suggestion of Hume's). This is quite different from the atheist's 'there is no God' (sense B).

One would indeed wish to say that everlasting existence is part of the concept of a God; of Hume's senile creator one would wish to say that since he is dead now he never was God when he was alive. But saying this does not commit us to the fallacy of the Ontological Argument. It belongs to the concept of a phoenix that it should never die by accident and should ward off old age with a bath of flames at regular intervals; so a dead phoenix is a contradiction in terms. But this does not mean that there must be a live phoenix. If there is a God, then he lives for ever; but we cannot determine from this whether there is a God.

Existence in sense C is, according to Aquinas, always existence in respect of some form: *quodlibet esse est secondum formam aliquam* (Ia. q.5 art.5 ad 3 um). For it is in this sense of 'exist' that we say a thing goes on existing; and for a thing to continue to exist is for it to be the same X over a period of time, where 'X' represents some *Begriffswort*; and this in turn means the persistence in an individual of the form expressed by the predicable expression 'X'. Thus, a man continues to exist in that the baby, the youth, and the grown man are *the same man;* and this means the persistence in some individual of the form, *Begriff*, that answers to the *Begriffswort* 'man'.

III

Having explained the construction of the phrase 'that by which . . .', and the relevant sense of 'is', we consider what is meant by phrases of the form 'that by which x is', 'x' being replaced by the name of an individual. Now it is the fundamental doctrine of Aquinas, repeatedly stated, that except when x is God, x is never identical with that by which x is. This doctrine is, I think intelligible in the light of our previous enquiry; but it is a most surprising doctrine. Why should we, how can we, distinguish between an individualized form and that by which the individualized form *is*? e.g. between the redness of Socrates's nose and that by which the redness of Socrates's nose *is*, goes on existing? We find in Aquinas himself remarks which might suggest the view that *esse* is an inseparable and only conceptually distinct aspect of the individualized form itself. '*Esse* of itself goes with a form, for form is actuality' (*Esse autem per se convenit formae, quae est actus*) (Ia. q.75 art.6); 'For any given thing, that *by* which it exists is its form' (*unumquodque formaliter est per formam suam*) (IIIa. q.2 art.5 ad 3 um).

All the same, I think there are good reasons for accepting the real distinction between an individualized form and the corresponding *esse*. The most important and most general reason is stated succinctly but clearly by Aquinas himself. If *x* is F and *y* is F, then in respect of F-ness *x* and *y* are so far alike; the F-ness of *x* will indeed be a different individualized form from the F-ness of *y*, but they will be, as F-nesses, alike. But when *x is* and *y* also *is*, the *esse* of *x* and the *esse* of *y* are in general different as such (Ia. q.3 art.5: *Tertio . . .*). Now this marks an unbridgeable distinction between *esse* and any form F-ness whatsoever. And the distinction between the references of the expressions 'that by which—*is*' and 'that by which—is F' will not vanish even if the *esse* of God and (say) the wisdom of God are identical; no more than 'the square of' and 'the cube of' have the same reference because 1 is both the square and the cube of 1.

A modern philosopher will often challenge philosophical assertions with the question: As opposed to what? This is a legitimate move; as Aquinas says, knowing the truth of an assertion is tantamount to knowing the falsehood of its contradictory opposite (Ia. q.58 art.4 ad 2 um). Well then, as opposed to what does one say that in general the *esse* of *x* and the *esse* of *y* are as such distinct?—In the fairy-tale, all the human members of the family and the family cat shared a single life, that is, a single *esse* (*vivere viventibus est esse*); and when the betrothed of the youngest daughter took a pot-shot at the cat, its death was the death of the whole family. In actual families, animality is common to all the members of the family, including the cat, but *esse* is not, and so killing the cat has no such consequence. So, although for a man or cat to go on existing is precisely the continued existence of his animality, that is, the persistence of a certain individualized form in continuously renewed matter: nevertheless we must recognize a real distinction between his animality and his *esse*.

A second reason appeals to the nature of intensive magnitude. It may be that *x* is F and *y* is F, and that they have the same specific F-ness, but yet the F-ness of *x* is more intense than that of *y*. Moreover, the F-ness of *x* may become more or less intense; and increase of F-ness plainly resembles a thing's coming to be F, whereas a decrease of F-ness resembles a thing's altogether ceasing to be F. Now difference between *x* and *y* as regards intensity of F-ness is not difference precisely as regards F-ness (especially as we may suppose *x* and *y* to have the same specific F-ness); it is rather, I wish to say, difference as regards the existence of F-ness—the F-ness of *x* exists more than the F-ness of *y*. So also a change in mere intensity is a change as regards existence; increase in the intensity of *x*'s F-ness resembles the coming to be of *x*'s F-ness, both being additions of existence; decrease in the intensity of *x*'s F-ness resembles the ceasing of *x*'s F-ness, both being subtractions of existence. Here again, there is a real distinction between the F-ness of *x* and the *esse* of this individualized form; while the F-ness as such remains unchanged, its existence may vary in degree.

(I have deliberately stated this argument in a schematic way, in order to avoid irrelevant controversy about my choice as an example. It is not so easy as it looks to find an unexceptionable case of difference or change in mere intensity, without any difference or change in quality: Aquinas's favourite example, heat, would land us in many difficulties. So far as I can see, *sound* is a good example. A louder and a softer sound may be qualitatively identical; and a sudden increase of loudness resembles a sound's suddenly starting, a sudden decrease of loudness its suddenly stopping.)

A third reason is found in considering the nature of thought. How remarkable that if there can (logically) be an X, there can also be a thought of an X! What is this relation *being a thought of*, which can have anything whatsoever as its term—even non-existent things like dragons? And how can there be an activity whose whole nature consists in its having this relation to something—to 'something' possibly non-existent?

Now Aquinas's account of thought denies that its nature

consists wholly in relation to something outside itself. When Plato thinks of redness, what exists in Plato is not a certain *relation* to redness or red things, but *is* redness, is an individual occurrence of the very same form of which another individual occurrence is the redness of this rose. But how then is it that this rose is red but not Plato's mind? Because the *mode* of occurrence of redness—not the redness that occurs—is unlike; the redness in Plato's mind *is*, exists, in a different way (*esse intentionale*) from the redness in this rose (which has *esse naturale*). We thus understand the intimate connexion of thought and its object. There is, as Aquinas often says, *likeness* (*similitudo*) between them. We also now understand the odd-seeming fact that there can be a thought of anything that there can be. Existence makes no difference to, and can impose no restriction on, the nature of that which exists; if it is possible that there should be F-ness at all, then it is possible alike that there should be F-ness occurring with *esse naturale* (a real live cow, say) and that there should be F-ness occurring with *esse intentionale* (a thought of a cow). The whole basis of this account is that the individual F-ness is really distinct from its *esse*, *naturale* or *intentionale* as the case may be.

To get this doctrine of Aquinas's properly straightened out in our minds we must realize that Aquinas is not saying e.g. that the cow in the meadow leads a double life and has another *esse* in my mind; or that I, when I think of the cow, become somehow identical with the cow. These kinds of talk (derived, I should guess, from taking too seriously the notorious trick expression 'in the mind') are expressly rejected by Aquinas. 'A stone is *not* in the mind (*anima*), it is the likeness (*species*) of a stone that is there . . . the similitude of a thing thought of (*intellectae*) is a form in the understanding' (Ia. q.85 art.2). There is one individualized form in the stone, and another individualized form in the mind of the man who thinks of it; these individualized forms are both occurrences of the same form, but differ in their manner of *esse*; neither the stone nor its individualized form is to be found in my mind.

Even when one angel thinks of another, what is in the knower is an individualized form differing from the individualized form that is in (or rather, for Aquinas, is identical with) the angel who is known, although both are occurrences of the very same form. On Aquinas's view, the difference (say) between Michael's thought of Gabriel and Gabriel himself, like the difference between my thought of a cow and the cow in the meadow, consists in one and the same form's occurring in Michael (or me) with *esse intentionale*, in Gabriel (or the cow) with *esse naturale*; and this involves the existence of two individualized forms (Ia. q.56 art.2 ad 3 um). It should be noticed in regard to the last citation that the difference between *esse naturale* and *esse intentionale* can occur even when there is no question of matter; angels, for Aquinas, have no sort of matter in their make-up, but the difference still holds good in their case.

I have had to be brief and leave out many important topics: in particular, the difference between the nature or essence and the (substantial) form of a material thing; the sense in which the human soul is the 'form' of the human body; the conception of *materia prima*; the question whether angels are 'forms' (sc. individualized forms). Even so I could not make this paper easy going, nor avoid what many people would call hair-splitting distinctions. But all serious philosophy *is* difficult; and as for hair-splitting,

> A Hair perhaps divides the False and True,
> Yes; and a single Alif were the clue—
> Could you but find it—to the Treasure-house
> And peradventure to THE MASTER too.

5

What Actually Exists

Existence in the sense of actuality (*Wirklichkeit*) is several times over emphatically distinguished in Frege's works from the existence expressed by 'there is a so-and-so' (*es gibt ein*—). Indeed, he says that neglect of this distinction is about the grossest fallacy possible—a confusion between concepts of different level. Actuality is attributable to individual objects; the existence expressed by 'there is a—' is not. When we ask whether there is a so-and-so, we are asking concerning some *kind* of objects whether anything at all *is* that sort of thing; and we cannot ever sensibly affirm or deny existence, in this sense, of an individual object, any more than we can sensibly ask whether a *thing*, rather than a kind of things, is frequent or infrequent. This doctrine of Frege's seems to me clear and certain; and attacks on it seem to me to contain obvious fallacies, and often, to show an aversion to the clarity that logic can bring. I shall in this paper take it for granted that Frege was right.

Frege had less to say about existence in the sense of actuality; for he was interested in the foundations of mathematics; and the objects of mathematics, as we shall see, if they *are* objects, are not actualities. A provisional explanation of actuality may be given thus: x is actual if and only if x either acts, or undergoes change, or both; and here I count as 'acting' both the inner activities of mind, like thinking and planning, and the initiation of changes in things. This explanation coincides pretty well with the criterion of existence given in Plato's *Sophist*; Plato of course did not make Frege's distinction regarding existence.

I do not think this explanation or criterion can be developed into a definition. For it is not yet clear what counts as a thing's undergoing a change; when Plato counts *being thought of* as a change undergone by the object of thought, most of us will feel that he is playing a trick, whether or not he also deceived himself. We certainly could not count a thing as actual because it undergoes such a bogus change as coming to be thought of. I shall return to this difficulty later; and I shall then argue that the notion of actuality is needed to explain the difference between genuine changes, like the butter's melting, and bogus changes, like the butter's rising in price, and therefore cannot be itself defined in terms of change. All the same, my explanation is likely to be some use; for many of us have some intuitive grasp of this difference between real and bogus changes.

ON TALKING OF OBJECTS, ACTUAL AND NON-ACTUAL

On the face of it, we are committed to recognizing As as a kind of object when we use the logical apparatus of identity and quantification along with the word for an A: in the vernacular, we do this by using such locutions as 'any A', 'each A', 'some A', 'the same A', 'another A', 'just one A', 'three As', 'that A which', 'all those As which'. I broadly agree with Quine on the matter; such disagreements as have previously appeared in print are not here relevant. I further hold that this commitment is only a defeasible one; a thinker may in fact defeat his commitment if he can show, or at least sketch, a method of paraphrasing away the ostensibly identifying and quantifying language he uses about As. But he cannot get out of his commitment by simply refusing to recognize it—by pronouncing a ritual disclaimer, 'I do not believe in such mysterious objects as As'.

With this criterion of ontic commitment, we may see that the ordinary language of arithmetic and geometry does *prima facie* commit us to recognizing numbers and geometrical objects as kinds of objects that there are. We recognize them as kinds of objects, by using the apparatus I have described; and as kinds of objects that exist, by using assertorically such locutions as 'There is a number which . . .' or 'There is a point which . . .'.

Now it would clearly be absurd to ascribe to numbers any actual, genuine, change; and it would be superstition if one seriously ascribed to numbers thoughts and plans and the initiation of changes (say, in human fortune). So if there are such objects as numbers, they are non-actual objects. And geometrical objects also would have to be non-actual; for nothing *happens* in geometry—the dramatic language about 'rearing' and 'dropping' and 'cutting' is only a teaching device, to catch the wandering attention of pupils.

The feeling I have that there *cannot* be such non-actual objects is a very strong one; according to a story Wittgenstein once told me, Frege too had this feeling from time to time. But like Frege I am unable to bring out what I feel in a definitely formulated difficulty. Talk of 'mysterious entities' gets us nowhere. Is not man a mystery? And the criterion of identity for a man is certainly not less problematic in philosophical debates than the one for a number or a straight line. Moreover, we should be very unwise to hope some definite contradictions will show that designations of numbers and geometrical entities are not genuine designations. Elimentary Euclidean geometry was shown by Tarski to be a decidable system, so it is certainly consistent. For elementary number theory, after Gödel, the position is not so happy but it would surely be silly to sit waiting for some inconsistency to turn up, like a vengeful Mrs. Boffkin. The tricks you can play with 'o' certainly do not show that this is not a name of a number, in the way the tricks you can play with 'nobody' and 'somebody' show that these are not names of persons. Numbers self-applied, as in a sentence beginning 'There are six perfect numbers between six and . . .', might seem to risk inconsistency; but none has ever been shown to arise.

I have no space to discuss attempted demythologisings of

arithmetic and geometry; I can only say dogmatically that so far they have been very complicated and obscure, and it is very doubtful whether they work. For example, I cannot imagine why somebody to whom points and lines are *entia non grata* should be willing to accept Whitehead's *Ersatz*— classes of infinite Chinese-box series of solids, or something of the sort; set theory, to put it mildly, has no better founded an antology than elementary geometry. So for the time being I see no way to avoid commitment to non-actual objects. A further consideration is that I do not know of any coherent finitist logic, which would impose an upper limit on the lengths of formulas and proofs; but the ontology of the syntax-language for infinitist, i.e. ordinary, logic is a theory tantamount to elementary number theory. I can only conclude with Tarski's epigram: *Inimicus Plato, sed magis inimica falsitas.*

This does not mean that any old theory of non-actual objects is unexceptionable. General set theory has to be a theory of non-actual objects; for its requirements could not be met (a point Frege made against Schröder long ago) if one regarded a set, even of actual concrete objects, as a whole compounded out of its elements. (And it makes no difference to the structure of set theory if we read the epsilon as meaning '—partakes in the Form —'.) Now general set theory escapes paradoxes only by arbitrary and unintuitive restrictions; so a certain measure of scepticism appears justified. And we ought to be still more sceptical about abstract entities for which no clear criterion of identity is provided at all, like meanings, attributes, and pieces of information (Frege's *Gedanken*).

SUBSTANTIAL AND ACCIDENTAL ACTUALITY

When I say 'This table is square', what I say latches on to the table; but does it, more particularly, latch on to an actual entity distinct from the table—the squareness of the table? Again, if the cat is on the mat, does this involve that some actual entity—a fact or complex or relationship—is describable as 'the cat's being on the mat'?

Such accidental entities as I have just mentioned played a prominent role in scholastic philosophy, and also, under a different style, in Cambridge philosophy between the two wars. I shall not try to settle the question at issue; I shall just state some points *pro* and *con*.

Against recognizing such accidental actualities, the same point may be made as against recognizing some sorts of abstract entities: there is in general no coherently stated criterion of identity, or there are rival criteria that give rise to a spurious-seeming problem of deciding between them. For which interpretations of '*F*' and '*G*' do '*x*'s being *F*, and '*x*'s being *G*' represent the same fact, or the same accidental form? How much worse the situation is here than for 'the number of *F*s' or 'the class of all *F*s'! Again, is Solomon's being the son of David the same fact, the same relationship, as David's being the father of Solomon? Or are we to say, with Aquinas, that in one man there is only one (natural) paternity, so that David's fatherhood is what makes him both father of Solomon and father of Nathan? On this latter view, since Solomon and Nathan are two sons of David, there are two distinct sonships involved, Solomon's and Nathan's; and neither of these is the same relationship as a fatherhood in David—they are specifically different from it, as two cars are from a dog. (See *Summa Theologica* IIIa q.35 art.5.) Now how can the issue between McTaggart (say) and Aquinas on the identity of relationships possibly be settled? What consideration could be relevant? Hobbes might say: If this is not the philosophy and vain deceit that the Apostle warned us against, what is?

There is a more positive reason for rejecting such accidental entities. The phrases that serve to describe them are what grammarians call nominalizations, derived in a specifiable way from clauses—e.g. 'David's fatherhood' from 'David is a father'. It therefore seems worth investigation whether we cannot reword sentences containing such nominalizations so that the corresponding clauses appear instead; and in many instances it seems that we can. The reworded sentences will tempt us much less to a postulation of accidental entities. 'The redness of Smith's nose is a result of drink' seems to predicate something of an accident or fact, the redness of Smith's nose; but no such appearance is generated by 'Smith's nose is red because he drinks'.

There are, however, some phrases ostensibly designating accidental individuals that it is much harder to get rid of in a plausible way. 'The top surface of this box is black.' The initial noun-phrase here is not easy to regard as a nominalization of 'The box is top-surfaced' or the like; nor is it easy to see how this sentence and 'black' can be fitted together in some syntactically coherent string tantamount to the original sentence (and there is the further difficulty that 'black' is clearly a first-level predicate of actual objects). Similarly for 'The hole in the tooth was smaller than the dentist's finest probe'; can we rephrase this, using 'The tooth was holed'?

As I said, I shall not try to answer the problem of this section; rather, I shall move quickly on to a specially important case of it.

CONTINUANT AND OCCURRENT ACTUALITY

'Socrates walked and then he ran.' If this, said in a suitable context, is a true proposition, does it relate to just one changeable actuality, Socrates? Or does it also relate to two occurrent actualities, Socrates' walking and Socrates' running? Or, finally, does it relate only to the two occurrents commonly called 'Socrates' walking' and 'Socrates' running'? Is 'Socrates' a mere convenient bit of jargon for talking about a lot of occurrent individuals, as 'the average man' is for talking about a lot of individual men?

The last of these three suppositions was long popular, and was elaborately expounded and defended, but I shall say very little about it. I see no reason whatever to try to construct a language in which the only things we can refer to are occurrents, not the people and things of ordinary discourse (including, of course, ordinary *scientific* discourse, which freely refers to experimenters and pieces of equipment). And I see no reason to expect that ordinary discourse will be paraphrasable into this hypothetical language.

'Paraphrasable in principle, of course!' Well then, I'm waiting to hear the principle that requires this: it had better be a good one.

There is much more to be said for refusing to recognize at all such occurrent individuals as Socrates' running; for sentences that contain a phrase like 'Socrates' running' can nearly always be easily turned into ones that contain instead 'Socrates is running' or some other tense of this. And for occurrents, as for accidental entities generally, there are perplexing and absurd-looking questions of identity. We are inclined to say that two different and logically independent narrative propositions may report one and the same past event—'I gave the grocer a £5 note', 'I paid my debt to the grocer in full'. But then, what is the criterion of identity for the event? Often, I am afraid, we have not the vaguest idea; this would explain the maddeningly sterile discussions about identity between mental and cerebral events. (Of course it is quite useless to stress that the identity in question is *strict;* this merits the retort I once heard of, that a neo-Pythagorean would have just as much right to say: 'The moral predicates of Justice and the mathematical predicates of Four are certainly different; but all the same, Four and Justice are strictly identical, and have both sets of predicates'!)

On the other hand, there are certain recalcitrant words and phrases for occurrents that resist this attempt to replace noun-like descriptions of events by narrative propositions. It would be very troublesome, for example, to have to replace 'He uttered the sound *bek*' by something like 'He beed, and then he eh'd, and then he kayed'. Sounds are on the face of it actual individuals that can be directly identified and counted.

A further reason why one should count occurrences among actual individuals comes out when we consider a problem about change that was mentioned before. The only sharp criterion for a thing's having changed is what we may call the Cambridge criterion (since it keeps on occurring in Cambridge philosophers of the great days, like Russell and McTaggart): The thing called 'x' has changed if we have '$F(x)$ at time t' true and '$F(x)$ at time t^1' false, for some interpretation of 'F', '*t*', and '*t*¹'. But this account is intuitively quite unsatisfactory. By this account, Socrates would after all change by coming to be shorter than Theaetetus; moreover, Socrates would change posthumously (even if he had no immortal soul) every time a fresh schoolboy came to admire him; and numbers would undergo change whenever e.g. five ceased to be the number of somebody's children.

The changes I have mentioned, we wish to protest, are not 'real' changes; and Socrates, if he has perished, and numbers in any case, cannot undergo 'real' changes. I cannot dismiss from my mind the feeling that there is a difference here; and I suggest that when we have a narrative proposition corresponding to a 'real' change, there is individual actuality—an imperfect actuality, Aristotle calls it—that *is* the change; but not, when a *mere* 'Cambridge' change is reported. (Of course there *is* a 'Cambridge' change whenever there is a 'real' change; but the converse is not true.) But it would be quite another thing to offer a criterion for selecting, from among propositions that report at least 'Cambridge' change, those that also report 'real' change (given they are true); and I have no idea how I could do that—except that I am certain there is no 'real' change of numbers.

Another sort of occurrents that I am disposed to recognize as actualities are mental acts, like thoughts. For McTaggart these were so clearly actual that he speaks of them as 'parts of the self'—where nobody would be tempted to call the softening of the butter a *part* of the butter, even if we recognize it as a 'real' change of the butter. McTaggart was very indiscriminate, I think, in his use of the term 'part'; but I think too that he was after something important. I cannot here try to follow this trail further.

DO THINGS TAKE TIME TO BE ACTUAL?

If some occurrents are actual entities, then clearly the answer is yes; sounds take time to be actual, and so do 'real' changes. What about continuants? Well's Time Traveller asks if we can conceive of an instantaneous cube. If 'cube' is used in the geometrical sense, then it is perfectly easy to think of a cube without temporal duration; as I said, nothing happens in geometry, and time just does not enter. But suppose we think of a sugar cube! A kind of stuff, like sugar, is characterized by the specific things it does and has done to it; could there be sugar for a shorter time than it takes for these specific activities to occur? This question is closer to natural science than many philosophical questions; for it suggests that care may be needed in asserting the existence of an unstable chemical compound or sub-atomic particle for a *very* short time; if the time is *too* short, the assertion may become incoherent, because the thing might be supposed to exist for a time that would not allow its characteristic behaviour. As Aquinas said, that *is* a given thing which performs the operations of the thing; the thing does not, then, exist if the relevant operations *cannot* exist.

ACTUALITY AND ETERNITY

There is no manifest contradiction if we suppose that some actual being has thoughts and designs, and initiates changes in things, but does not itself undergo changes initiated by other things. (I am here naturally considering only 'real' changes, not mere 'Cambridge' changes that are not 'real'.) Such an actual but unchanging being could fairly be called eternal.

Could it, though? Would a changeless being whose duration co-existed with that of changeable beings be anything more than a temporal being whose successive states were alike rather than variegated?—I deny the right to speak of 'successive states' in regard to such a being. For how would the states be differentiated? Perhaps it will be said: By relational properties; if a changing being has various states, then one state of the unchanging being will co-exist with one state of the changeable being and another with another state, and this will be enough to differentiate the states of the unchanging being. But once again, I deny that there are any 'states' of the unchanging being to be differentiated. My imaginary opponent is held captive by a picture: some such picture as a uniform blue line with a graduated ruler laid against it, so that we can discriminate successive bits in the blue line. But time-order (as I have argued elsewhere)[1] is categorically different from spatial order; and any such picture is limited in usefulness and profoundly dangerous. Nothing is sillier than to think you can settle philosophical problems about time by drawing diagrams.

Theologians may protest that God's eternity cannot be adequately conceived as absolutely changeless actuality. No doubt all our conceptions of God are most inadequate; but that does not mean they are false. And if someone says that God's eternity is something simply out of relation with what occurs in time—that we ought not to say e.g. that God lived *before* the world came into existence—then his view is probably confused and certainly unscriptural. 'Before the mountains were brought forth, or ever thou hadst formed the earth and the world, from everlasting to everlasting thou art God.' 'Before Abraham was, I am.'

I suspect some theologians of wishing to replace this conception of an eternal God, whose changeless duration co-exists with and overflows the duration of mutable things, with the conception of a God who is changeless because *not actual.* Surely it is for this reason that we hear so much of its being wrong to say God *exists;* for this reason, that Tillich emphatically repudiates the idea of a God who acts —who 'brought the universe into existence at a certain moment, governs it according to a plan, directs it to an end'.[2] Well, I suppose people can worship the non-actual, as Pythagoreans worshipped the number Four; but it is excessively misleading if they claim to be worshipping the God of Judaism and Christianity. And for myself all their words count for no more than the sly whisper of Eric Ambler's mad professor, 'The cube root of two is God'.

[1] 'Some Problems about Time', *Proceedings of the British Academy,* 1965.
[2] *Systematic Theology,* vol. ii, p. 6. I owe this reference to John Passmore's *Philosophical Reasoning* (Duckworth, London, 1961), p. 49.

6

Causality and Creation

People once used to believe that there are deductive causal demonstrations of the existence of God. The proof of God's existence was supposed to be deductive, in the sense of being valid according to generally accepted rules of logical deduction; causal, in that it had among its premises propositions about things being caused; and demonstrative, in that it proceeded from indubitable premises (e.g. 'Some things come into existence') and therefore must if valid reach an indubitable conclusion. People who believed this had no place for ideas of our needing a special sort of reasoning not paralleled elsewhere (perhaps performable only by a 'baptized reason'), or perhaps needing a special non-logical intuition, in order to grasp the truth of God's existence.

In our time there is a general impression that attempting a deductive causal demonstration of God's existence is a plain absurdity like trying to square the circle; this is supposed to have been proved somehow. Sometimes people think modern logic has shown that in a deduction you can only bring out what was already contained in the premises, so that an argument to prove God's existence must beg the question. This objection, which I shall consider later, would touch all deductions, not just deductions of God's existence.

Again, many people think Hume has proved something about causality which makes a causal demonstration of the existence of anything an impossibility. Surprisingly enough,

75

people who think this hardly ever ask themselves what the logical form or forms of causal propositions may be; and yet it ought to be obvious that if someone alleges that a certain sort of conclusion cannot be reached by reasoning that uses premises of a given logical form, then he can make good his allegation only if he rigorously specifies this logical form. Until that has been done, there is no reason to suppose that Humean objections have any weight.

Hume himself had no conception of logical rigour; he lived in the middle of a barren patch in the history of logic and this may excuse him; but it does not excuse our contemporaries who follow him in his logically sluttish ways and make no attempt to apply well-known logical techniques. You find admirers of Hume giving 'A causes B' or 'A is caused by B' as the schema of a causal proposition; they are quite likely to explain that 'A' and 'B' represent expressions for events, but they are not at all likely to say whether these expressions would stand for kinds of events or would have singular reference to individual events—they do not feel it matters. But of course if we do not know whether the allowable interpretations of the schematic letters are to be general or singular terms, the logical work required has not even been begun. In the circumstances, a Humean's assertions as to what logically can or cannot be done by causal arguments are just gratuitous.

The traditional sort of causal proof referred to examples of causality among things in this world, and went on to conclude that there is a God who causes all these things. This feature too now raises difficulties against such a proof. It has long been said that the term 'cause', like other terms, is used only analogously of God and of things in the world. From this it has sometimes (I think quite mistakenly) been inferred that any mention of the sort of causality that occurs within the world is out of place in an argument to prove the existence of the First Cause. If this inference were correct, there would once more be a fatal objection to deductive proofs of God's existence from causal premises; for if the premises contain no mention of ordinary causality, but use 'cause' in a special sense that applies only to God, knowing the premises to be true would involve already knowing that there was a God, and the deduction could not profit anybody.

Faced with this difficulty, some people have argued that we cannot demonstrate God's existence in the sense of proving it from premises, but only in the sense of pointing out, to a metaphysical eye that has somehow been got open, the dependence of finite being on the Infinite or of contingent being upon the Necessary Being. I cannot make any sense of this metaphysical vision; neither, I suspect, could Aquinas—I find no mention of it in his works, where indeed the term 'metaphysical' rarely occurs, and no place for it in his commendably pedestrian theory of the natural working of the human mind. Certainly this understanding of 'necessary' and 'contingent' is quite alien to his thought; for him contingent beings are beings liable to corrupt, break up, or the like, and necessary beings are beings with no such inner seeds of their own destruction; souls and angels belong to the latter class, and so, he thought, do the heavenly bodies, which, being supposedly incorruptible, are expressly called *entia ex necessitate* (Ia q.115 art.6).

My own view is that at least the first three of the five 'ways' both were intended to be logically conclusive and may possibly, on suitable restatement, in fact be so. The general arguments against using deduction can, I think, be quite easily refuted; whether the first three 'ways' are valid can be determined only by considering them, not by including them in some blanket condemnation. But I am afraid logic is not yet in a position to pronounce decisively on their validity, because the formal logic of causal propositions, which was studied a little in the Middle Ages, has made no progress to speak of since then; it was not included in the miserable mutilated torso that passed for the whole body of logic from about 1550 to 1847, and since then the interest of formal logicians have been so predominantly mathematical that they have quite neglected causal propositions, which of course are not needed in mathematical reasoning.

I shall say something by way of preliminary to a formal logic of causal propositions; may others push the work on.

There are in the first place objections to the whole idea of proving God's existence by deductive methods; these would, if valid, make it a waste of effort to examine any alleged deductive proof in detail. But they are not valid. Naturally it is no objection to an alleged deductive proof that if it is valid its conclusion follows from its premises— that is just what makes it valid; but some people think there are necessary features of deductive proof which makes it useless for theology. Let us take P to be the premise and Q the conclusion of a deductive argument; we can always reduce the case of several premises to that of a single premise by forming the conjunction of those premises. We are commonly told such things as that if Q follows from P but not vice versa, then P is stronger than Q, more questionable than Q, and harder to verify than Q. These are clearly intended to be substantial assertions, to the effect that where a one-way relation of deducibility holds, some other relation holds; and the holding of this other relation is somehow supposed to make the proof trivial and ineffectual.

In fact, the first two of the above assertions are empty tautologies, from which nothing follows about proofs of God's existence or anything else. To say that if P logically implies Q but not conversely, then P is (logically) stronger than Q is to say nothing; for 'P is stronger than Q' is just another way of saying that P logically implies Q but not conversely. Again, to say that P is more questionable than Q is to say that if we answer the question whether Q is true in the affirmative, then this does not yet commit us to answering affirmatively the question whether P is true, but a negative answer to the first question does require a negative answer to the second; this is once more just a long-winded way of saying that Q follows from P but not vice versa; so we are told nothing in being told 'If P logically implies Q but not conversely, then P is more questionable than Q'.

Failing a clear and coherent account of verification, which I shall believe somebody can produce only when he has it available for criticism, I cannot do much with the asssertion 'If P implies Q but not conversely, then P is harder to verify than Q'. But this last formula is irrelevant to our enquiry unless its consequent clause at least implies that it is harder to get to know that P is true than that Q is true, supposing they both are true. Now this relation need not hold between P and Q when Q follows from P but not conversely; it is harder to know the truth that there is no greatest prime number than to know the truth of the premises from this theorem follows. I dare say somebody will protest that these premises, unlike those used in a causal proof of God's existence, are all purely *a priori*. But, though Wittgenstein once thought otherwise, we need the same set of rules of inference no matter whether the premises are empirical or mathematical; so there is no reason to doubt that even outside mathematics a conclusion is sometimes less easily known than the premises from which it logically follows.

A great illusion is here produced by speaking of a validly drawn conclusion as contained in the premises. This metaphor would be useful if there were some generally effective technique by which the information given in the premises could be actually displayed as containing that given in the conclusion. For some parts of logic there exist such effective procedures; and when Wittgenstein wrote the *Tractatus*, it was a reasonable conjecture on his part that this held good for logic as a whole. However, new discoveries may falsify seemingly well-established assumptions; and it is now definitively proved for wide domains of logic that there is no such effective procedure for exhibiting a conclusion as an excerpt from the premises. We can philosophize about this result, but we cannot philosophize it away; and in the circumstances the metaphor of 'containing' is thoroughly misleading.

In syllogistic, as Aristotle already knew, there are effective decision procedures for validity; so it has some point to say that in arguing syllogistically we are only pulling out of the box what we first put into it. But, whatever Kant and some neo-scholastics have thought, syllogistic is only a small fragment of logic; and objections that rule out a syllogistic proof of God's existence do not necessarily rule out deductive proofs.

It is in fact very easy to show that a valid deductive causal proof of God's existence could not possibly be purely syllogistic. We might suspect this, for such a proof could hardly avoid making essential use of e.g. the fact that some causal relation is transitive and aliorelative, and thus overstepping the bounds of syllogistic. However, the matter admits of formal proof. In a valid syllogism the truth-condition for each premise and for the conclusion will consist in whether some complex general term or other applies or not within a certain universe of discourse—the same universe for premises and conclusion. This comes out when we use such diagrams as Venn's or Lewis Carroll's to test for validity. If, therefore, the universe of discourse involved in the premises is the familiar universe of mutable things, no syllogistic manipulations can bring out a conclusion asserting the existence of something not belonging to that universe—an immutable God. You cannot possibly defend both the exclusively syllogistic character of logic and the deductive nature of natural theology; and the sooner this is realized the better.

Even those who hold that logic is not purely syllogistic sometimes quite fail to realize the qualitative difference made by the introduction of relative terms into our reasonings. In all of syllogistic we need consider only one-place predicates and what we can form from them with 'and' and 'not', i.e. their Boolean functions; and a Boolean function of predicates never gets us out of the universe of discourse of those predicates. But if we form a general term with the relative term 'smaller than' and the general term 'visible' which both apply to members of the directly observable universe, the term 'smaller than any visible thing' can have no such application, and if it applies at all it applies outside the logical limits of that universe. To quote Quine: 'Such a compound . . . does not even purport to denote things to which we could point and give individual names if they came our way. The relative term "smaller than" has enabled us to transcend the old domain, without a sense of having fallen into gibberish. The mechanism is of course analogy, and more specifically extrapolation' (*Word and object*, p. 109).

Now obviously what does for 'smaller than any visible thing' goes for 'cause of every mutable thing'; so long as 'cause of' and 'mutable' have application within our familiar universe, we may introduce the term 'cause of every mutable thing', and reason as to what other predicates this term implies, without a sense of having fallen into gibberish— even though this term could not itself apply to anything within the familiar universe. Such reasoning will indeed as Quine says involve analogy and extrapolation, but that need not frighten us. *Per Deum meum transilio murum*—by my God I leap over the wall.

I shall now make some remarks about causal propositions. Logical analyses of causal propositions are I think a necessary prerequisite if we are to examine causal arguments. Of course they would not be necessary if we could accept the general view that deductive proof is anyhow cognitively valueless, since then the peculiar logical structure of a proof would not signify; but I see no reason to accept that view.

I believe there are at least two distinct, though related, types of causal propositions. (A) We have the type often put in the form '—is the cause of—', where the blanks are filled up with abstract-noun phrases; often with phrases that would be taken to designate events, but by no means always. Examples:

> The motorist's high speed was the cause of the crash.
> The camber of the road was the cause of the crash.
> The motorist's lack of due care and attention was the cause of the crash.

We pretty plainly have here what Ryle called systematically misleading expressions. For one thing, speaking of 'the' cause is calculated to ensnare people—as it does—into pseudo-problems as to which of the factors mentioned was really the cause of the crash. Moreover, if we take seriously the grammatical appearance that the abstract noun-phrases we have here are designations, we shall have on our hands an intractable lot of individual entities standing in causal relations, for example an individual which *is* a lack of due care and attention. To call such individuals queer would be mere rhetoric; I called them intractable because they have no principle of individuation, no criteria of identity; what individuates the particular lacks of due care and attention?

Our only hope of clarity in dealing with (A)-type causal propositions is to recast them in the canonical form of the medieval logicians' causal 'hypotheticals', 'p because q' or 'because q, p'. In these schemata, the letters go proxy for clauses, not for abstract noun-phrases. Our previous examples would become:

> The motorist crashed because he drove fast.
> The motorist crashed because the road had such-and-such a camber where he was driving.
> The motorist crashed because he was not at the time carefully attending to his driving.

There are many unsolved problems about this connective, 'because'; but I suggest we cannot even begin to discuss (A)-type causal propositions with profit unless we first throw them into this canonical form.

(B) There are propositions asserting efficient causality, of the form 'x caused y to be an A', or, more generally, 'x brought it about that p'; where 'x' and 'y' are schematic letters going proxy for singular designations of individuals (of self-subsistent ones—*actiones et passiones sunt suppositorum*) and 'A' goes proxy for some predicate, and 'p' as before for a proposition.
Examples:

> Phidias caused the block of marble to be of human form.
> Phidias brought it about that the block of marble had human form.

I am very uncertain about the relation between (A) and (B) types of causal propositions. It is however obvious that we need a sound account of (B)-type propositions if we aim at logically analysing causal proofs of God's existence; for the intended conclusion of such proofs is that something, which we call God, causes to change everything that does change and brings into being whatever comes to be. This sort of proposition is obviously derived quantificationally from a (B)-type causal proposition.

The quantification of my (B)-type propositions is of importance in another way too: it enables us to show the difference between God's creating an A and his making something to be an A—something presupposed to his action. We may insert an existential quantifier to bind the 'x' in 'God brought it about that x is A' in two different ways:

(I) God brought it about that (Ex) (x is an A)
(II) (Ex) (God brought it about that x is an A)

(II) implies that God makes into an A some entity presupposed to his action; but (I) does not; and we express the supposition of God's creating an A by conjoining (I) with the negation of (II), for some suitable interpretation of 'A'. For Example:

God brought it about that (Ex) (x is a human soul in body b); and for no x did God bring it about that x is a human soul in body b

expresses the supposition that God created a human soul in b, and did not cause some entity x presupposed to his action to be the soul of the body b.

This analysis brings out various points that Aquinas makes about creation: e.g. that in creation the thing created does not undergo change, and is not passive to a divine action. We can further see how in creation there is no real relation of God to the creature. For God's creating an individual c would be expressed by a proposition of this sort:

There is just one A; and God brought it about that (Ex) (x is an A); and for no x did God bring it about that x is an A; and c is an A.

The part of this proposition that expresses the creative act namely the first three conjuncts) does not mention c, and explicitly denies that in creating God acted upon any individual.

The distinction between two ways of inserting an existential quantifier, which I have used to elucidate the difference between creating an A and making something to be an A, is not an *ad hoc* logical dodge to explain a dubious theological distinction; it is on the contrary well known to logicians who study what are called intentional verbs. For example, the sentence 'I am looking for a detective story' is ambiguous in an obvious way: in the vernacular, the difference would be explained somewhat as follows: 'I may mean just some detective story or other, or I may mean a particular detective story'; this explanation, though for some odd psychological reason it works, is logically lame, for any detective story you like is 'just' some detective story or other, and is also a particular detective story. What is intended may be got by two different ways of inserting an existential quantifier into the formula 'I am endeavouring that it may be the case that I find x, and x is a detective story' namely:

(III) I am endeavouring that it may be the case that (Ex) (I find x, and x is a detective story)

(IV) (Ex)(I am endeavouring that it may be the case that I find x, and x is a detective story)

The logical relationship between (III) and (IV) is exactly the same as that between (I) and (II). Just as I said (I) is compatible with the negation of (II), so (III) is plainly compatible with the negation of (IV). And just as 'God created an A' does not assert a relation of God to an A, so 'I am looking for a detective story' interpreted as (III) does not assert a relation of myself to a detective story.

The quantification in (IV) raises, indeed, some serious puzzles, which Quine and others have discussed; but the analogous puzzles in regard to propositions about divine action would relate not to (I) but to (II), that is not to God's creating an A but to God's making something into an A. The idea that creation involves insuperable logical difficulties, as compared with ordinary making, thus turns out to be unfounded; apparent difficulties often arise from illicit manipulations of the word 'nothing' in 'made out of nothing', but the idea of creation does not require that such manipulation should be legitimate. To be fair, I must say that nonsense about how nothing is the stuff we are made of is to be found in some Catholic writers, e.g. Dr. Sheed; but Aquinas explicitly warns us against this nonsense (Ia. q.43 art.1 ad 3 um, art.2 ad 4 um).

There is a lot more hard logical work to be done in these areas: but I hope I have said enough to show how empty the claim is that we know enough about the logic of causal propositions to see that there can be no causal deductive proof of God's existence. It may even be rational, as I am inclined to think it is, to accept some such proof as valid before a satisfactory logical analysis has been worked out: mathematical proofs were valid and rationally acceptable long before logicians could give a rigorous account of them. But especially in face of scepticism, a highly rigorous analysis of the proofs is an urgent task; and after all some accepted ways of mathematicians have turned out not to be logically acceptable. And a necessary preliminary to such analysis is a fully developed logic of causal propositions, which we need anyhow to deal with many non-theological reasonings.

I suppose I ought to say something in conclusion about the idea that it is somehow improper or irreverent to employ the rigour of logic in speaking of the Divine Majesty. To me it appears blasphemous to say God is 'above' logic; logic is named from the Logos, which was in the beginning with God and was God. In a Muslim story, a fallen champion saw a Crusader wielding against him a magic invincible sword bearing the name of God: 'Sword' he cried 'can you strike a true believer? Do you not know the name on your blade?' 'I know nothing but to strike straight', the sword replied. 'Strike then, in the name of God!' Logic is not partisan, and knows nothing but to strike straight; but the sword is invincible, bearing the Maker's name.

7

Praying for Things to Happen

Christians have a custom of praying to get things: not only supernatural things like grace and glory, but ordinary observable things like daily bread or recovery from sickness or success in an examination. I am not going to consider how this custom might be justified, or whether indeed it can be justified by reasons that do not presuppose Divine revelation; I shall confine myself to drawing certain consequences from the supposition that the practice is justified, and to answering some objections to the practice.

It is merely odd that some people have doubted whether this is a really Christian practice. I remember a philosopher affirming in discussion that the Lord's Prayer was an example not of the 'lower' sort of prayer in which one prays for something to happen but only of the 'higher' sort in which one expresses acceptance of the Divine Will. He was, however, clearly wrong, even if we forget the petition for daily bread. For 'Thy will be done' in the context of the Lord's Prayer is not expressing resignation; it is a petition that God's will may be willingly obeyed by the inhabitants of Earth as it is already by the blessed in Heaven; and like the rabbi in the Jewish story, we need only open the window to see that this Messianic hope is not yet fulfilled. Those who say it *is* fulfilled already are just uttering incantations, like Christian Scientists who say men are never sick or sorry.

I shall be concerned only with prayers for *ordinary* observable happenings. Miracles would of course by definition be observable; but the concept of miracle is very difficult, and anyhow I have no idea what to say on the question when it is right to pray for a miracle.

It is part of Christian tradition, not only that people ought to pray for things to happen, but also that they sometimes get things by praying for them; theologians call this 'impetration'. Moreover, belief in impetration by prayer can certainly not be reduced to the bare thesis that what people pray for sometimes comes about, and comes about by God's will as all things do; such a reduction would, for example, make a mockery of Christ's emphatic words about prayer in the Gospels. Even if the duty of petitionary prayer could be established by natural reason, I at least do not see how the impetratory role of prayer could be thus established. But Christians, who rely on the word of their Master, are confident that some prayer is impetratory: that God gives us some things, not only *as* we wish, but *because* we wish. I shall do my best to clarify these causal propositions, and to remove certain difficulties in the way of our accepting them.

The doctrine that prayer is impetratory must be sharply distinguished from a magical view of prayer. In Southey's poem the wicked Maharaja Kehama manages to sacrifice a hundred stallions in a ritually flawless way on a hundred successive days, and thereby makes it impossible for the gods not to grant his wishes. It is certainly not open to a Christian to think of impetration like that; nor need he feel himself pushed towards such an idea. It makes sense to approach God in the style of a petitioner only if one conceives of God as a rational agent who acts by free choice. Now if a rational agent does what is asked of him, this does not mean that he lacked freedom to have acted otherwise; yet we may truly say that he acted as he did *because* he was asked. To say that God brought something about *because* of a man's prayers is not at all to say that, once the prayers had been said, God could not but grant them; for this is not at all what we mean when we use similar language about petitions men address to other men.

Let us, however, consider a certain implication of this 'because' language we use about human granters of petitions. If a man would have done something, was going to do something, even unasked, then we cannot compatibly with this say he did the thing because he was asked. A father, let us say, has already decided to give his son a pony for his birthday, and so we can say he was anyhow going to give him a pony; we then cannot compatibly with this say that the father gave the pony *because* the boy asked for it. At least, this is not quite right; as was remarked to me, the father might have decided as follows: 'I'll give the boy anything he asks for, within reason; but if he doesn't ask for anything, I'll give him a pony'. In this case the two propositions could both be true—that the father would have given the boy a pony even if he hadn't asked for anything, and that the father did give the boy a pony because he asked for it. But even so we can say these two propositions are incompatible:

(1) The father was going to give the boy a pony for his birthday whatever the boy asked for or didn't ask for:

(2) The father gave the boy a pony because he asked for one.

It is this implication that raises difficulties about the impetratory role of prayer. In speaking of a human granter of petitions, I have been switching about between 'he was going to give' and 'he would have given', as though it were all one which expression I used. I think this is justifiable, but there are problems here; and for the moment I don't want to discuss how we can use tensed language about the eternal God, let alone such a philosophically puzzling tense as the past future, 'was going to'. (This is only a postponement; we shall find that in this discussion we cannot shirk the problems of tensed language about God.) But even if we stick to the 'would have' way of speaking, I submit that we get a straight incompatibility between 'God brought about situation S because of X's prayers' and 'God would have brought about situation S regardless of X's praying or not praying'. Or, to put this another way: 'God brought about situation S because of X's prayers' implies 'If X had not prayed, or had prayed otherwise, God would not have brought about situation S'.

The logic of such subjunctive conditionals is notoriously obscure. But one thing seems clear: from 'It could have been the case that p' and 'If it had been the case that p, it would have been the case that q' there follows 'It could have been the case that q'. Now whether and how a man prays is within his own power: in so far as this is not so, if a man cannot help praying—e.g. if he is hypnotized or brainwashed into uttering the words of a prayer, or if he utters them in some *brevis furor* of anger or fear—then the prayer just does not count as a prayer. But if the man had *not* prayed then God would not have brought about the situation S that he prayed for, and therefore S *would not* have come about. So S *could* have *never* come about; but also S *could* come about, because S did come about—the prayer was granted. The upshot is that if we are to be justified in saying that a state of affairs S came about from somebody's impetratory prayer, then at the time of the prayer S must have had two-way contingency: it could come about, it could also not come about.

The first and most obvious conclusion from this is that there can be no impetratory prayer in regard to things already past at the time of the prayer. The contrary opinion, along with various other theologically suspect ones, was held by Gerard Manley Hopkins. In his verse, at any rate—as he made plain in his explanatory letters to Robert Bridges—he had prayers for people not to have gone to hell, though he firmly believed it was no good praying for people already in hell:

> And that prayer thou hearst me making
> Have, at the awful overtaking,
> Heard: have heard and granted
> Grace that day grace was wanted.
>
> Not that hell knows redeeming,
> But for souls sunk in seeming
> Fresh, till doom-fire burn all
> Prayer shall fetch pity eternal.

I do not know Hopkins's prose remains, so I do not know whether he offered any rationale of these *ex post facto* prayers. Anyhow, such prayers relate to the granting of Divine grace, which as I said I cannot discuss here. But we find a rationale of *ex post facto* prayers expounded in C. S. Lewis's works, *The Screwtape Letters* and *Miracles;* and he is concerned with observable past issues, such as: whether my friend has come safely through some exposure to danger that is now over. Lewis argues that God timelessly sees the whole pattern of events in time and the whole pattern is subject to God's will: so God can shape an event that comes earlier to fit in with a prayer that comes later.

Fortunately we need not discuss the mysteries of God's eternal knowledge and power in order to see that Lewis's theory will not do. For it is not a matter of what God knows or can do, but of what we in prayer can sensibly say. If a prayer does not make good sense, then equally it does not make good sense to speak of God's granting it. And a prayer certainly does not make sense if we try to use a past tense of the imperative mood and pray that a state of affairs *may have* come about. In using the imperative we represent the situation as still to be brought about, and in using the past tense we represent it as already a *fait accompli* one way or the other. These representations will not fit together; such a prayer makes no better sense than a schoolboy's prayer for π to have the value he gave it in his maths test—3.1416 or 3 1461, as the case may be.

Lewis admits that it is no good praying for a thing not to have happened when we know it has happened; for in that case we should be setting our own will against God's will as manifested in the actual issue. But if my own objection to praying about the past is a sound one, then it is not a matter of our ignorance, any more than it is a matter of God's omniscience. A prayer for something to have happened is simply an absurdity, regardless of the utterer's knowledge or ignorance of how things actually went; just as the prayer for π to have a certain numerical value is absurd, whether or not the schoolboy has learned the actual value of π after doing the test.

I am not arguing that an imperative in the perfect tense never occurs in ordinary language or is necessarily meaningless. As Hopkins pointed out in a letter to Bridges, this would be quite wrong; we get such an imperative when a tutor says to his pupil 'Have your essay written by Tuesday morning'. But this does not make sense of the sort of imperative that would be used in praying about the past. The indicative corresponding to the tutor's imperative is 'You will have written your essay by Tuesday morning'; and this is not in the past tense. It is in the tense aptly called by old grammarians *'paulo post futurum'*: it relates to a time somewhere between the time of speaking and the following Tuesday morning—and thus to a time which is future, not past, when the tutor speaks, though by the Tuesday morning it will be a past time.

Now suppose the tutor had said: 'Have your essay written by last Tuesday morning'. The undergraduate could make no sense of this; there is no coherently constructible indicative to correspond. For 'You will have written your essay by last Tuesday morning', read so as to correspond to this imperative, implies a contradictory time-specification, of a time which is both future at the time of speaking and past by the previous Tuesday morning. And it is equally incoherent to pray to God 'Let my friend's aeroplane not have crashed last Tuesday morning'—supposing that I've just learned my friend was flying that day, but have not learned whether he landed safely. No doubt God, who knows our necessities before we ask and our ignorance in asking, sometimes does in his mercy do *something* about the most confused prayer; but there's no sense in saying he *grants* such a prayer.

Lewis more than hints that time does not exist 'from God's point of view' but only exists 'from ours'; in *Miracles* he has a parable of a designer who can see a whole pattern of lines on a piece of paper as simultaneous, whereas to the consciousness of a given line in the pattern the various bits of the pattern appear as successive. This way of talking is quite common in popular theology, and it is important to see why it will not work. If time does not exist from God's point of view, if God sees all things as simultaneous, then there are only two alternatives. First, that God is unaware of the temporal aspect of things, which is so important to us; much as the God of Empedocles (if we may trust Aristotle's *Metaphysics*) was wholly unaware of Strife, which men know only too well. I need not linger on this alternative. The other alternative is that things really are all simultaneous, just as God sees them to be, and that our consciousness of things as successive is a misperception. Lewis seems to favour this alternative; but it is equally inadmissible.

Even if a man's impressions as to which realities are past, present, and future are illusory, the fact that he has in that case different and uncombinable illusions shows that at least his illusions are really successive—that they are not all present together, but now one illusion is present and now another. Whether entities A, B, and C really are events in succession or are only misperceived as being such, if an observer has the experience of remembering A, perceiving B to happen, and expecting C, and also has the experience of remembering that A happened before B happened and perceiving C, then these two experiences of the observer are uncombinable, and cannot occur in him simultaneously, but only successively. But in that case temporal succession itself cannot be an illusion, since the so-called illusion of successiveness is already a real succession of experiences: just as misery cannot be an illusion, because to be under the illusion of misery would be real misery. Parmenides and Mrs. Eddy alike can neither deny nor fit into the universe what they call 'the error of mortal mind'.

Even if there were not decisive reasons for rejecting as logically incoherent the theory that time and succession do not exist 'from God's point of view', we should still need to notice that no Christian apologist can use this theory. For the one thing that is clear about Divine creation is that the things created have to be temporal, even if the Creator and his creative act are held to be eternal. If time is an illusion, then there is not the sort of mutable world that can be supposed to be a creation; so in this case the Judaeo-Christian doctrine of creation has to be rejected. Significantly the doctrine *was* rejected by great metaphysical thinkers, Spinoza and Bradley and McTaggart, who denied the reality of time. And again, if time is an illusion, this strikes at something that is central to the Christian creed: its reference to a datable event in time—the crucifixion of Christ under Pontius Pilate.

I am not saying that God is changeable, that he has different information available at different times; but I am saying that God sees creatures *as* changing and *as* being in different states at different times, because that is the way things are and God sees things as they are. Moreover, though God's knowledge is unchangeable, *we* have to use different propositions at different times in order to say *what* God knows. As Aquinas remarked, it is wrong to say 'Whatever God once knew he does know', if the 'whatever' relates to propositions (*enuntiabilia*); for example when Socrates was sitting it was right to say 'God knows Socrates is sitting', but it is wrong to say this now if Socrates is no longer sitting.

Similarly, though the arm of the Lord is not made short, it is false to say 'Whatever God was able to bring about he still is able to bring about', or 'Whatever prayer God could have granted he still can grant'. For though whatever state of affairs is conceivably accomplishable can be accomplished by God, nevertheless when once a situation belongs to the past, to the region of *fait accompli*, it no longer comes under the notion of the conceivably accomplishable. Here, as in regard to what God knows, the change involved is a change in creatures not in God.

It is idle and vain, then, to pray concerning an issue envisaged as past; we can sensibly pray only concerning future contingent issues, where things still can go either way. (It is irrelevant that a past issue once was contingent, if we know that it is now decided and there is no longer any contingency about it.) The contingency of what we may sensibly pray for arises because it is foolish to try to obtain by prayer what is either impossible or inevitable; we sensibly pray for S when S may yet come about because our prayer impetrates it, though S may also not come about—after all, our prayer does not magically constrain God.

Now a future issue cannot be thus contingent if, miracles apart, it is already determined in its causes. I said at the beginning of this paper that I don't know in the least when one ought to pray for a miracle; let us rather consider an issue, say the result of an examination, about which it would not be justified to pray for a miracle. Suppose the examiners have completed their formalities and are bound by university statutes to make no further alterations: then the result is determinate in its causes, and at this stage it is unreasonable to pray with a view to affecting the issue, if one knows things have got thus far. We may reasonably pray about the weather if we regard the weather as future contingency; but astronomical events are already determined in their causes, and if we are not praying for a miracle it is senseless to pray about sunsets or eclipses.

The distinction I have just drawn, between issues already determined in their causes and contingent issues, was of course regularly drawn by medieval philosophers. The actual place where they drew the line was fixed by obsolete Aristotelian physics and astronomy. But the distinction itself was sound; at least, so it appears to me.

Men of science have indeed often asserted that 'in principle' the movements of the stars and of the atmosphere are on the same level of predetermination, and that the appearance to the contrary is just our ignorance. Well, they've kept saying this since Queen Victoria's days; but a Shropshire farmer still acts with good sense if he treats the weather forecast on the radio a bit less seriously than the time of sunset printed in his diary. As for the matter of 'principle': even in principle the weather is not predictable from material causes, for it is notoriously affected by the voluntary actions of men; the rainfall of the Holy Land, for example, has been affected by its deforestation in past centuries under the Arabs and its reafforestation under the Jews. So there is not the least reason to distrust the *prima facies* of contingency in the weather.

This is, of course, by no means the only example of *prima facie* contingency. And there is solid reason for believing that the appearance is not delusive. Upon the whole, men's conjectures as to the ways of things in the world—e.g. as to the laws of motion, the nature of the stars, the shape of the Earth, the interactions of substances, the workings of the human organism—have begun by being extremely wide of the mark and have long continued to be so. But now consider what happened when a serious theory was first devised for the kinds of events that have immemorially been reckoned as chance events. The theory of probability arose, Voltaire tells us, from a problem posed by an *homme du monde* to an *austère Janséniste*. The Chevalier de Méré, a seasoned gambler, had observed that there is a slightly worse than even chance of getting a double six in twenty-four throws of a pair of dice, but a slightly better than even chance of getting a six in four throws of a single dice. Pascal's calculations, based on assumptions about equal possibilities, exactly agreed with this experience.[1] Again, being kicked to death by a horse is just what people would count as a matter of luck, bad luck of course: and during the lifetime of the Hohenzollern Empire German cavalrymen perished in this way strictly in accordance with the laws of probability. People will account for such facts by a vague idea that 'it's logically bound to work out in the long run'. This supposed logic, as Von Wright has elaborately proved, is a tissue of fallacies; anyhow, the fact to be explained is agreement in the *short* run—that is what makes probability theory practically important; in the long run we are all dead, like the Hohenzollern Empire and its cavalrymen.

There is massive evidence, then, that classes of events that would naively be counted as chance events really do conform

[1] I am told it was Fermat, not Pascal; this spoils Voltaire's epigram, but not my argument.

to an *a priori* standard of contingency, in which now this, now that, possible alternative is realized. Such events, a theist may hold, are in truth not determined by any created causes, but do not on that account escape the order of Divine Providence. 'Lots are cast in the lap: but they are disposed of by the Lord.' Our reason, seeking a pattern in chance events, is able to find one even there, because these events too fall under the order of the Divine Reason of which our own is a faint reflection.

The empty claim that all events in the material world are determined in their causes and are 'in principle' predictable has had a deplorable influence on Christian apologetic; although men of science today are less confident about this claim than a man like Tyndall was, the mischief has already been done by their predecessors. It is often held with absolute certainty that events in the material world (at any rate large-scale events) are determined in certain created causes, so that (to use C. S. Lewis's example) the fair weather at the evacuation of Dunkirk was determinate at the formation of the solar system. Sometimes this certainly is based on a superstitious belief in the predictive feats of science—really, of course, a physicist cannot predict how dice will fall any better than I can. Sometimes, people appeal to a supposed metaphysical truth, 'the principle of causality', which is alleged to rule out two-way contingency. Those who thus swear by 'the principle of causality' are rarely forthcoming with any attempt at an exact statement of it; but I well remember one of them having a shot at this in discussion, and coming up with a formulation essentially like Spinoza's, which had the undesired consequence of ruling out all free choice, Divine as well as human.

We often find Christian apologists committing themselves to strict determinism as regards the material world (at least in its large-scale aspects) and then by consequence to the desperate task of explaining how God, while 'binding Nature fast in fate Left free the human will'. *Pace* Pope and Leibniz, I think the thing cannot be done. If Nature is bound fast in fate, then the human will is a chimera buzzing in a vacuum and feeding upon second intentions. How can I have any freedom of speech if the sound-waves impinging on your ears as I speak are determined in material causes going back to the origins of the solar system and having nothing to do with my thoughts and intentions? It is indeed a presupposition of rational human action that there should be a great deal of determinism in the material world; otherwise, as the Warden of Keble has remarked in his Gifford Lectures, we should be like Alice trying to play croquet with a live hedgehog as a ball and a live flamingo as a mallet —both creatures having 'wills of their own'. But equally we could not play croquet if the balls moved like stars in their courses regardless of the players' wishes and plans.

I argued that the impetratory role of prayer requires large-scale two-way contingency in the observable world. But this is no difficulty against Christian belief if we have good reason to admit such contingency anyhow, as I have argued that we have. There are many large-scale future events in the physical world which are contingent in regard to all created causes, and which we cannot predict (even leaving aside the possibility of miracles) from consideration of any created causes; there has to be this element of chance in things if human choices are to have any *Spielraum*, as they manifestly have. But such contingent events do not fall outside the order of Providence, which can arrange them so as to answer prayers. Whether and when prayers are so answered, it is not for philosophy to say.

My final problem concerns certain tensed propositions about the Divine will that need to be discussed in connexion with prayer. When we are speaking of a man who grants petitions, we may say pretty well indifferently 'He was going not to bring about S'—having regard to a time before the petition—or 'He would not have brought about S'. Can we use the past-future form with regard to God? To take a Bible example: can we say that God was going not to let Ezechias live (as indeed the Prophet Isaias declared to him) but that God in fact restored him to health because of prayers? I am not at all sure what the right answer is.

The obvious objection to this way of speaking is that it would involve that God's will is changeable. If it was first true to say 'God wills that King Ezechias should not recover' and later true to say 'God wills that King Ezechias should recover' then surely God's will must have changed. But really the inference is not obvious. If we are to affirm God's changelessness (and I think there is very good reason to do that) then we must reject as invalid certain inferences about God's knowledge and power similar to this one about God's will. If God's knowledge is to be changeless, then a pair of premises like 'It was once true to say: God knows that Socrates is sitting down' and 'It is now no longer true to say: God knows that Socrates is sitting down' must not imply that God's knowledge has changed. If God's power is to be changeless, then we must not be allowed to infer a change in God's power from the premise that 'God can stop Miss X from losing her virginity' was once true—before she was debauched—and is now true no longer. (I take this example, like the one about God's knowledge, from the *Summa Theologica*.) But if we disallow these inferences, we may equally disallow the inference from 'God was not going to let King Ezechias recover' and 'God did let King Ezechias recover' to a change in God's will. Traditional theology explains that the apparent change in God's knowledge or power is really a change in the creature, Socrates or Miss X, not in God: may not the apparent change in God's will be likewise explained away as a change in Ezechias? For Ezechias, as men say, was first of all in such condition that he was not going to recover, and then he did recover; and his condition, first and last, was by the will of God.

Theologians, again, are wont to say that God's will is necessary 'in its entity, but not in its term': that is, that propositions about what God wills in the created world are not necessarily true. But at that rate one might equally say that God's will is unchangeable 'in its entity, but not in its term': that is, that propositions about what God wills in the created world are not unchangeably true. And surely we must say this; even apart from the matter of King Ezechias; for

'God wills to bring so-and-so about' can no longer be true when *so-and-so* is already a *fait accompli.*

I am well aware that we cannot hope in this life to resolve all such problems; but part of our difficulty here arises not from the mystery of God's eternal life, but from our inadequate concept of change. The only sharp concept of change that we have is what I have called the Cambridge concept:[1] viz. that A changes if of two propositions about A, relating to different times but otherwise alike, one is true and the other false. If the Cambridge concept were adequate as well as sharp, then each pair of premises that I have said does *not* imply a change in God *does* imply such change. But even in its application to creatures the Cambridge concept is clearly inadequate; for by that concept Socrates would change if Theaetetus grew and became taller than Socrates, or even if some schoolboy came to admire Socrates in the twentieth century. These, we should wish to say, are not *real* changes in Socrates. But I do not know of any criterion, let alone a sharp one, that will tell us when we have a *real* change in Socrates and not just a 'Cambridge' change. The search for such a criterion strikes me as an urgent task of philosophy; even if you think philosophical theology is chimerical, this task is worthwhile for the general light we should gain about time and change if the search were successful; and in Christian dogmatic theology too a sound concept of real change would be a powerful tool. But I must end with this because I do not know what to say.

[1] See Essay 5.

8

On Worshipping the Right God

People whose attitude to the truth about God is altogether frivolous often remark that after all we all worship the same God; if these were the only people who said so, the remark would hardly deserve attention. It is all too clear that they are only evincing their unwillingness to bother themselves; just as they will also make the equally dubious assertions that we are all going to the same place when we die or that we shall all know someday. But the thesis that all *bona fide* worshippers worship the only God, 'in spirit and in truth', has found worthier advocates, for example Tolstoy; and in these oecumenical days some people are willing to hold this about at least some faiths quite alien to the Judaeo-Christian tradition, the 'great religions'.

This sort of oecumenical spirit is quite opposed to the teaching of the Scriptures, and to the great bulk of Christian tradition. The Old Testament has consistently vituperative language about worship of the Gentiles' gods—'lies, lying vanities, whoredom, abomination, shame of the filth', etc. Apart from the Apocalypse, the New Testament writings are less vituperative; but they are not a bit more friendly. There is not a hint that *bona fide* worship of a heathen god does the worshipper the least good; on the contrary, we read that the worshipper is alienated by his ignorance from the community of the true Israel and from the life of God. So far from being told that the heathens worship the true God, we read that what they worship is a *nothing*. And most Christian tradition, within the communion of Rome or outside it, is to the same effect.

I shall be expounding and defending this common Christian tradition. To begin with, we must consider what it is to give somebody or something divine worship, *latria*. First, nobody is worshipping something as God if his worship does not rest in the thing itself, or in some deity supposedly indwelling in the thing, but passes on to something else that the thing represents or recalls. People who have professed themselves unable to see the distinction only showed themselves to be at best obtuse; for they would readily see that burning a man's effigy or a country's flag with public execration is an act of dishonour that does not rest upon the object burned but goes on to the man or nation that the object is associated with.

It is more difficult to show the rationale of the distinction for which Roman theologians used the contrasted labels *latria* and *dulia*. A philosopher of my acquaintance once said, 'It sounds like this: you go down on one knee to Our Lady but on both knees to God.' But of course in some societies this might be the very thing to show which sort of honour one was paying to somebody, *dulia* or *latria*; the rule might be that you knelt on one knee to the King when presented at Court but on both knees when praying in the temple; and then a king who demanded that his subjects kneel on both knees might intend, and be understood to intend, a blasphemous claim to divine worship. Again, in old Mexico, if we may rely on Prescott, incense was burned merely as an act of courtesy to guests; but in the Mediterranean lands for many centuries this was a sign of *latria*, which the Christians had to refuse to the Emperor.

In these instances, the distinction between *dulia* and *latria* is relative to established customs; but it is not always thus relative. The institution of sacrifice, though it takes various forms, is very recognizable in cultures in which it occurs; and whenever it occurs, it is an act of *latria*; for it expresses God's eminent domain, as lawyers say, over all that we have and are. Again, only God may be asked for pardon of sin; as the psalm says, 'To thee only have I sinned'; for it is God whose law men break, God alone who reads the sinner's heart, and God alone who can pardon. Again, if grace is conceived as an incipient partaking in the Divine Life, and glory as intimate union with God in knowledge and love, then petitions to obtain grace and glory may rightly be addressed only to God. To offer sacrifice, or to pray for mercy and grace and glory, is of its nature an act of *latria* —an act of worship that may lawfully be paid only to the true God.

I shall not discuss whether the practice of praying to the saints is justified; at all events, it is clearly not an act of *latria*. This is shown for one thing, by the fact that the saints themselves are being asked to pray to God; for another, by the difference in style of address shown for example in the Roman litanies—'pray for us' to the saints, 'have mercy upon us' to the Divine Persons. Again, in some liturgical prayers of the Roman Church, God is asked to effect something by the intercession of the saints— the underlying doctrine being that it is only by sharing in God's knowledge that the saints so much as know what someone desires by their intercession and only by the guidance of the Holy Ghost that the saints know what to ask for.

There is, then, a world of difference between a well-instructed Christian who prays to the saints as intercessors and a heathen polytheist who notionally acknowledges a supreme God but in the practice of his religion prays only to inferior deities. The heathen regards the supreme God as too remote for his prayers, and then seeks benefits from the inferior deities; but those Christians who pray to the saints are well aware that 'our God is very close to us' and that they have the *parrhesia*, the freedom of speech, to call God their Father. I do, however, find something decidedly heathenish in that poem of Gerard Manley Hopkins which assigns to the Blessed Virgin the role of keeping God's terrible glory at a safe distance, just as the air we breathe keeps off the rays of the sun that would otherwise prove lethal. He seems to have felt relief that God was less close now to the Christians than God had been to the Jews!

I have tried to distinguish *latria*, the form of honour or worship that is due to God alone; it now ought to be clear that sometimes *latria* is paid to inappropriate objects instead of to the true and living God. For one thing, there is idolatry: divine worship paid to a human artefact. (This narrower use, which I shall here maintain, seems to me clearer than the wider use, in which any misdirected *latria* is called idolatry.) People have thought, and I fear still do think, that it is psychologically impossible for anyone to regard an inanimate artefact as a present deity and not just as a symbol. This is rather like the idea of the Victorian rationalists that the practice of witchcraft is not merely ineffectual but non-existent; in spite of anthropologists, this latter idea still oddly survives. Both ideas involve an exceedingly strange combination of beliefs as to what lies inside and what lies outside the limits of human folly; it is held that men are not silly enough ever to have gone in for such-and-such a practice, but are silly enough to have thought the practice was widespread when in fact it never existed at all. I doubt whether such a combination of beliefs is consistent; anyhow, in both instances, the idea was quite wrong—both witchcraft and idolatry are well within the limits of human folly.

Idolatry takes two forms, a more primitive and a more sophisticated. The primitive form is like what I remember a psychologist's calling *dollatry*—the attitude of many a young child towards her dolls. In a way she may know the dolls are inanimate, but as she plays with them she makes believe—she half makes herself believe—that the dolls have life and sense. Certainly there is no question of her even half believing in a spirit distinct from the doll that sometimes enters into it and manifests itself. I have not much to say about idolatry on this childish level; we may well hope that in God's eyes such idolators are no more responsible than children, even when they are cruel as children often are; but of course this does not dispense us from the duty of trying to bring them to knowledge of the truth.

At the more sophisticated level, the god who is worshipped is distinguished from the image, but is believed to be specially present in the image. It is this more sophisticated idolatry whose existence people are strongly inclined to deny, but, I repeat, quite wrongly. Aquinas quotes some typical passage from the Hermetic writings expressing this idolatrous belief; and I myself read, in a Hindu propaganda magazine for Western consumption, an explanation of how after proper priestly consecration of an idol the Godhead enters into it, so that the Infinite becomes circumscribed, the Source of life inanimate, the Omnipotent helpless, the Omniscient insensible—so great is the Divine condescension!

Another form of misdirected worship is the worship of heavenly bodies as living gods. This has been found in highly sophisticated and civilized societies, like those of Babylon and Athens. The Athenians wanted to kill Anaxagoras for the blasphemy of saying that the Sun and Moon were no gods but lifeless lumps, one hot and the other cold; Plato in the *Laws* has sophistical proofs for the divinity of the heavenly bodies, and regulations for a Nocturnal Council that would imprison such heretics as Anaxagoras and brainwash them into conformity.

We are not likely to be attracted, I think, either to Hindu idol-worship or to astral worship; they may well strike us as absurd and degrading, and I shall argue that this impression is right. But we in the West cannot afford to be complacent about idolatry. It may creep in even into the worship of the true God. In a tract I once read about the miracles of the Holy Infant of Prague, this image was supposed to have shown itself in a vision to somebody with its arms broken, and to have said, 'Give me back my hands and I will bless you.' If we had to believe that the Lord of Glory had spoken thus, the arm of the Lord would be shortened indeed. A more serious matter, in my view, is the way many people are coming to believe that 'thinking machines' *really* think and that we shall soon be able to build ones that think far more wisely than men. This superstition, if it spread, could lead to a far worse mental slavery than the heathens' idol-worship and consultation of oracles.

Both in the Old and in the New Testament, idolatry is spoken of, not just as an abomination in God's sight, but as a manifest folly. The sacred writers seem to assume that even by ordinary human reasoning a man not corrupted by an idolatrous environment can see the folly of idol-worship. And indeed it appears very arguable that the foolishness of idolatry is one of the easier conclusions of natural theology.

Natural theology is nowadays rather blown upon: I shall not directly defend it, but I shall seek to rebut certain objections to it in principle. A man may *assert* that God is too high a subject-matter for human argument; but having said this he had best keep silence, for if he *argues* the matter he at once contradicts himself. And if anyone seeks to praise God for being 'above mere logic', I reply, in Aristotle's words, *phortikos ho epainos*, the praise is vulgar: it is like the vulgar admiration felt for a 'genius' or 'great man' because he is 'above' the restraints of 'mere' courtesy and decency and honour. Indeed, in his work *The Idea of the Holy* Rudolf Otto tied up the awe we feel before a supra-rational God with that we feel before a 'daemonic' man of destiny.

If, as natural theology claims, we can establish by reason the existence of a Being whose will causes all that exists and all that happens in the world—'and this all men call God'— then the nature of a particular finite body is utterly disparate from the Divine Nature thus conceived. Every body undergoes change, and causes change in other things only by itself undergoing some change; whereas the Divine Nature, the cause of all things in the cosmos, must itself be conceived as changeless. Otherwise, God would just be one of the mutable things within the cosmos, and not the cause of them all.

This sort of reasoning has in fact been formulated quite independently of the Judaeo-Christian tradition.

> Mind is infinite and independent and is not mixed up with anything; it is alone by itself. If it were not alone by itself, it would have a bit of everything in it, and the things mixed with

it would have hindered it, so that it would not rule anything the way it does being alone by itself. For it is the finest and purest of all things, and it possesses all knowledge of everything, and is greatest in power; and Mind controlled the cosmic rotation, so that things began to rotate in the beginning. . . .And the things that were to be, and those that have been and now are no more and all things that are now, and the things that are to be—all these Mind has set in order.

So wrote Anaxagoras; I know the pundits say his conception of Mind was 'materialistic', but I very much doubt if they know what they mean, and on the face of it there are far more 'materialistic' expressions about God in Holy Writ.

This so far would only establish that the Divine Nature is incorporeal: it would not of itself exclude the possibility that the Deity should have some special union with, or presence in, an idol or a heavenly body. Nor must we exclude this possibility for the wrong reason. Some superior persons are of opinion that an infinite God cannot be any more present in one part of creation than in another; but this reason against idolatry and astral worship is certainly wrong. God is more present in rational creatures that bear his image than in irrational creatures, and among rational creatures some are more united to him than others. But this very truth points up the folly of idolatry; how can anyone believe that God is more specially present in the inanimate idol than in the worshipper himself, who bears God's image? A man is at any rate capable of some union of mind and heart with God; in a graven or molten thing God can be present only in a far inferior mode.

The same goes for the heavenly bodies. There is not and never has been the least reason to believe they are even alive, let alone intelligent; they deserve *latria* even less than a bull or a cat does. The contrary belief is mere superstition; and the arguments that Plato and others have used to defend it are discreditable rationalizations of this superstition.

The reasons I have sketched to show that idolatry and astral worship are follies cannot be turned against Christian belief in the Incarnation. Of course I do not think that natural reason can establish even the non-contradictoriness, let alone the truth, of the Christian belief that a certain human being was and is Almighty God in person—that, in the word of the carol,

> This little Child he made all things
> And this little Child is King of all Kings.

A demand for a strict proof of non-contradictoriness is anyhow often unreasonable—even, as recent logical researches have shown, in pure mathematics. Certainly, if the doctrine of the Incarnation is true, it will not be self-contradictory, and any argument that it is self-contradictory will in fact contain a flaw; but saying this is very different from saying that if the doctrine is true we ought to be able to see, or prove once for all, that it is non-contradictory. Nevertheless, as I have said, we do know that the mind and heart of a human being can in measure be united to God; this does not show the consistency of the doctrine that a certain human being is personally God, but it does show that that doctrine is not open to the same objections as the belief that an idol or a planet is specially indwelt by Deity.

A special difficulty, though, arises about the dead body of our Lord, and again about the Holy Eucharist. I fully accept the theologians' teaching that the dead body of Christ was still united to the Godhead; in the Apocalypse, he who says of himself, echoing Deuteronomy, 'Behold I live for ever', also says 'I became a corpse' (*egenomēn nekros*). But Christ's flesh was an integral part of that humanity which had been united to the Godhead and was predestined to be reunited with the Godhead forever at the Resurrection; it was therefore in quite a different case from an idol or a planet. The case is quite different, again, for some detached and now permanently inanimate part of Christ's body; to worship an alleged relic of this sort as if it had some still-inherent Godhead would be a perversion of the same sort as heathen idolatry.

As regards the Holy Eucharist, anyone who believed that a priest could effect a special and direct union of the Godhead with bread and wine would be no better than a heathen. But, for all the unhappy divisions of Christians about the Sacrament of Unity, I do not think such a view has ever been held. All Christians who take the Eucharistic rite seriously regard it as effecting a union of the worshippers with the redemptive acts of the man Christ Jesus; the question is then once again one of how God was in Christ, not of how God is in bread and wine. As Dr. Johnson said, 'Sir, there is no idolatry in the Mass; they believe Christ is there and they worship him'.

I have so far tried to characterize *latria*, and I have discussed idolatry in the narrow sense and astral worship. In these forms of *latria*, the worshipper worships something non-existent—an imagined Divine presence in, or union with, an inanimate object. An idol, said the Apostle, is *nothing*. But suppose a man does not thus vainly worship the inanimate, and does conceive himself as worshipping God; then does it follow that he must be worshipping the right God, the only true God?

It may be thought that since there is only one God to worship, a man who worships a God cannot but worship the true God. But this misconceives the logical character of the verb 'to worship'. In philosophers' jargon, 'to worship' is an intentional verb. The metaphor behind 'intentional' (*intendere arcum in*, to draw a bow at) may be helpful to remember; for of course one may shoot at an animal that is not there to be shot at. Similarly, a man may admire a non-existent author—as in some famous hoaxes people have been induced to do—or love a *princesse lointaine*. The idolator too (at least of the more sophisticated sort) is better described as worshipping the non-existent (an imagined special Divine presence) than as worshipping an existent but unworthy object, a stick or stone.

It is here important to notice that the term 'God' is not a proper name but a descriptive term: it is like 'the Prime Minister' rather than 'Mr. Harold Wilson'. Our indication of this is the fact that one translates the word 'God', as one translates the words 'Prime Minister', into a foreign language, whereas 'Mr. Harold Wilson' would be merely transcribed or transliterated. But this argument runs into trouble, because it is not always clear what is a translation or a transliteration. Is 'Warsaw' a transliteration of 'Warszawa', although it neither looks nor sounds quite the same? or is it a translation from Polish into English? And 'Deutschland' certainly is not transliterated by 'Germany'; and one might argue that it is on the contrary translated by 'Germany', since this would certainly be the word used in an English translation of a German text containing 'Deutschland'. (Unless indeed we had some other use of 'Deutschland'—e.g. as the name of a ship—when again it would be simply transliterated.)

There is, however, another related fact that points to the same conclusion. When St. Augustine and his companions landed in England they found the English paying *latria* to Woden, Thor, and other imaginary beings, to each of whom they applied the word 'God'; and the missionaries taught them not to apply this word any more to Woden and Thor and the rest, but solely to the Blessed Trinity. Similarly in other missionary countries. This makes it clear that in the mind of the Church the word 'God' is not a proper name, as the word 'Woden' was meant to be, but a descriptive term, true of the Blessed Trinity and not true of Woden. 'God' is a descriptive term; and in this life we know God not as an acquaintance whom we can name, but by description.

From this fact, and from the intentional character of the verb 'to worship', some important conclusions follow. I shall approach these by way of some parallel cases. Suppose during an election a canvasser met with an aged working man who declared himself a firm supporter of Mr. Macmillan as Prime Minister—'he's a grand old Unionist, isn't he?'; it emerges, however, that this voter associates the word 'Unionist' with Trades Unions rather than the Conservative and Unionist Party, and is in other ways hopelessly conflating the attributes of Mr. Macmillan with those of the late Mr. Ramsay MacDonald. The canvasser may perhaps nevertheless not scruple to make him promise to vote for Mr. Macmillan's man; but clearly the aged voter is not really a supporter of Mr. Macmillan at all—the Prime Minister whom he supports has no being outside his own senile fancy. Though 'to support' is not always an intentional verb—not when one speaks of a strut supporting a building, or a policeman supporting a drunk on his way to the station—it is intentional when political support is in question, and the arrow may be aimed at an imaginary target.

Again, suppose Mr. Smith looks up from his *Times*, having just read the University news, and says to his wife 'That fat charlatan we met yesterday has just been made a Professor at one of the new Universities!' His wife gently replies 'You oughtn't to speak so uncharitably of Jack Izzard-Wye, dearest; and anyhow it wasn't yesterday, it was the day before.' We must notice here the difference between personal and impersonal uses of the verb 'to refer'. What Smith actually said would be true only if the Smiths had met, on the day before Smith's remark, someone correctly describable as fat and as a charlatan; and the definite description 'that fat charlatan we met yesterday' could not otherwise be said to refer to somebody. I myself have grave doubts as to the utility of calling the description a referring expression, even if it does describe somebody; I think Russell is much more right than Strawson about all this. But this is not of present concern. Whether the description is correct or not, and whether or not, if correct, we may say that *it* refers, there is no doubt that *Mr. Smith* succeeded in referring to Jack Izzard-Wye, even though he described him a bit wrong. We need not doubt that similarly people may succeed in relating their thoughts to the true God even though they have a partly erroneous view of his attributes —like the holy hermit mentioned by Augustine who thought God was of human shape.

However, there are limits to the possibility. Smith could not possibly convey to his wife a reference to Jack Izzard-Wye if he said not 'That fat charlatan we met yesterday', but 'that fine baby we saw last week'. At least, he could refer that way to Jack Izzard-Wye if the Smiths had some sort of family code; but this is an exception that proves the rule— for then e.g. *being a baby* would not be part of what was intended by the description. And if in his private thoughts Smith thought of a healthy baby pushed in a pram the week before, he logically could not be thinking this thought about Jack Izzard-Wye. That is, it is impossible, given the actual attributes of Jack Izzard-Wye, that a thought of the baby's being so-and-so should be describable as a thought of Jack Izzard-Wye's being so-and-so. Similarly, we seem bound to conclude, a sufficiently erroneous thought of a God will simply fail to relate to the true and living God at all. Where the line is to be drawn God only knows; but then it is God, not man, who has to draw the line; since I am not the judge, the *kritēs*, I can decline to state a criterion. But there surely is a line to be drawn, a line that God does draw; and in that case some people will fall the wrong side of it—alienated from the life of God by the ignorance that is in them.

In saying this I am not saying that such fatal ignorance of God must itself be culpable; though no doubt it some-times is—the idea that men are never culpable for opinions they hold is a dangerous mistake. Ignorance of God may be deadly even if it is itself inculpable; for only by turning to the true God can a man win grace and forgiveness, and his ignorance may prevent him from doing this, so that 'the wrath of God remains upon him', as the Gospel says. For the sins of his past life, 'he who does not believe is condemned already'.

But cannot love unite a man to God despite any amount of intellectual error? I do not think so. The most earnest protestations of loyalty to the Prime Minister by my senile voter could not alter the fact that the object of his loyalty, 'Mr. Macmillan', was not the historical Prime Minister but the mere creature of a senile confusion. And a man's love for a woman, however much it means to him, scarcely latches on to her if his acquaintance with her is extremely slight, if she is for him a *princesse lointaine*, if he has fantastic misconceptions of her actual characteristics.

There is indeed one relevant difference between managing

to refer to some man and managing to refer to God. If Mr. Smith thinks of Jack Izzard-Wye, or the senile voter thinks of the Prime Minister, then the person thought of may well neither know nor care, and will certainly have only very limited control over, the thoughts the other person has of him. But according to Christian belief God does care that men should know him, and to that end God both enlightens men's minds and directs their wills. If a man comes to worship a God because the true God 'calls and draws him', then certainly this worship will be directed towards the true God, however inadequately conceived.

I see no reason, however, to believe that if there is one and only one God, then *all* human worship of a God comes about because men are 'called and drawn' by God. If we are not to trust just any religious inspiration, but to 'try the spirits whether they be of God', then there arises the question of a criterion. If a man has once admitted that the way God is conceived in a particular form of worship is *extremely* different from the way he himself conceives of God, then it ought logically to be for him a matter of doubt whether both forms of worship *can* lay hold of the true God. Doubtless, worship inspired by God would lay hold of him; but men may still have good reason to say: This worship certainly does not lay hold of the true God and therefore cannot have been inspired by him. And of course people who believed in only one God very often said just this about the worship of other peoples.

The upshot is that we dare not be complacent about confused and erroneous thinking about God, in ourselves or in others. If anybody's thoughts about God are sufficiently confused and erroneous, then he will fail to be thinking about the true and living God at all; and just because God alone can draw the line, none of us is in a position to say that a given error is not serious enough to be harmful. Some nuclear physicists hold that any degree of human exposure to hard radiation is harmful; there is no safe and tolerable level; there is no saying who in particular will die of diseases like leukemia, but some people will die and the more hard radiation there is around the more people will die. Similarly, any degree of error about the Divine Nature is harmful; and though we cannot say who are irreparably harmed, the more error about God there is around the more such people there are going to be.

I have spoken before of natural theology as a means of exposing errors about God. But it has on the contrary been argued that a God whose existence and attributes were established by natural theology would not really be the same God as the true and living God of religious belief, that natural theology of its very nature lays hold of the wrong God, an abstract sort of God. This argument appears to me confused. Suppose that Sherlock Holmes established from his data both the existence of a murderer—i.e. that the case actually is one of murder—and some of the murderer's characteristics. Suppose the police later on arrested a man with those characteristics and found confirmatory proofs of his guilt: it would occur to nobody, I imagine, to distinguish between the abstract murderer of Sherlock Holmes's deductions and the real live murderer raging in his cell; surely nobody would wish to deny this plain statement of the case, that Holmes had abstract knowledge relating to a concrete individual.

If Holmes had not regarded the murderer as a man and a brother (as, in fact, Conan Doyle represented Holmes's attitude) but simply as the solution to an interesting problem, he might well deserve moral censure; but this would cast no doubt on the correctness of his deductions, and it would remain merely silly to say that those deductions related only to an abstract sort of murderer and not to a real murderer. Of course somebody who engaged in natural theology for the pleasure of exercising his wits in a difficult subject would be even more open to censure than I was imagining Holmes might be; but this is as irrelevant as in Holmes's case to an appraisal of the arguments, and has no tendency to show that those arguments lead not to the true God but to a false abstraction. Anyhow, I see no reason why natural theology should lead to such perversity; perhaps

Anaxagoras did worship Mind, not only deduce its existence —certainly he gave that impression to the simple people of Lampsacus, who put up an altar to Mind and Truth in his memory.

But even if a natural theologian correctly concludes to the existence of a God with attributes ABC, and those attributes do in fact belong solely to the one true God, we cannot be sure that in worshipping the God whose existence he has concluded to he is worshipping the true God. For along with these attributes ABC the natural theologian may ascribe to his God others which are not those of the true God. Thus, he may like Spinoza falsely believe that God produces all possible creatures, by a natural necessity of fully manifesting his infinite power; or, like many moderns, he may falsely believe that God *needed* to create a universe full of creatures in order that they, however inferior to him, might be there to love and be loved by—much as a lonely old woman crowds her house with cats. Was Spinoza, and are these moderns, worshipping the true God, or rather worshipping some vain phantasm, like my senile voter's Prime Minister?

It is not for us to answer such questions; enough to notice that they arise; and there is no reason to doubt that sometimes a natural theologian's errors may mean that he does not lay hold of the true God in his mind and heart at all. My senile voter might after all think of his 'Mr. Macmillan' as having certain attributes that did indeed belong to the late Prime Minister and to him only—say, being head of the British Government in 1961; and yet we may quite well deny that his support for his 'Mr. Macmillan' makes him a supporter of the real Mr. Macmillan.

This conclusion raises a difficulty. If the natural theologian *proves* the existence of a God, it can only be the true God, someone may argue, whose existence is proved; so how can the natural theologian's God *not* be the true God? This argument, however, presupposes that to the question 'Which God has been proved to exist—the true God or some other?' there must be some answer. But in fact the proposition 'A God exists' does not ascribe the attribute of existing to some God or other—thus, either to the true God or to some false God—but rather affirms that something-or-other has Divine attributes. Now a man may at once truly believe, or even know, that there exists a President of France, i.e. that someone-or-other is President of France, and have a quite mistaken belief as to who holds that position—he might even suppose it to be held by someone whose very identity was just a private muddle, like the muddle of the student who said that Poincaré was at once an eminent statesman and a great mathematician. And similarly there is nothing to stop a natural theologian, or anyone else, from at once truly believing or even knowing that the Divine attributes belong to something, and making a false ascription of those attributes to an inferior or phantom object.

The doctrine I have been advocating—that we dare not accept a tolerant attitude towards errors concerning the Divine Nature, because we are in no position to judge what level of error will entail that a man's worship is wholly misdirected—has been used in the past to justify savage persecutions. But it is a disreputable argument against a doctrine to say that belief in it has had bad practical consequences: heavier-than-air flying machines and hydrogen bombs were after all possible, even though we should arguably have all been far better off if people had continued to believe them impossible. Moreover, a strong sense of the dangers of religious error does not commit one to thinking that 'the thumbscrew and the stake to the glory of the Lord' ever was really a good way of eradicating error; there is high authority to the contrary—our Lord's words of rebuke to the Apostles when they wished to see the obstinately heretical Samaritans burned alive (a passage of Scripture which the Church of England happily used in the thanksgiving service for the failure of Gunpowder Plot).

The right way, surely, is that of the missionary who counts no labour too great to win men from the Kingdom of Darkness. That burning love of souls is what charity means; charity is not, as people often think nowadays, a fatuous amiability towards every vagary of misconduct and misbelief. And it is again not charity, but impudent and detestable pride, to say that poor ignorant people may as well be left practising idolatry, because that is all they are capable of and God will expect no more of them in the way of worship. It is bad that some Christians should be indignant at Popish idolatry; but such misdirected indignation is very likely a more Christian attitude than amiability towards Papists on the part of a man who doesn't think idolatry matters anyhow, and would be equally amiable towards Priapists.

9

The Moral Law and the Law of God

In modern ethical treatises we find hardly any mention of God; and the idea that if there really is a God, his commandments might be morally relevant is wont to be dismissed by a short and simple argument that is generally regarded as irrefutable. 'If what God commands *is not* right, then the fact of his commanding it is no moral reason for obedience, though it may in that case be dangerous to disobey. And if what God commands *is* right, even so it is not God's commanding it that makes it right; on the contrary, God as a moral being would command only what was right apart from his commanding it. So God has no essential place in the foundations of morals.'

The use of this argument is not confined to a recent or narrowly local school of philosophers; it was used by the British Idealists when they dominated British philosophy, and, as we shall see, it was used much earlier than that. Nor is its use confined to people who do not believe in God; on one occasion when I attacked the argument, my chief opponents were not atheists but professing Christians. This is not surprising; for the argument was used by Christians of an earlier generation, the Cambridge Platonists, as a stick to beat that dreadful man Hobbes with. (I shall have more to say about Hobbes later on.) And they in turn got the argument from Plato's *Euthyphro*.

Let me summarize that dialogue. Euthyphro and Socrates
are discussing the trial in which Euthyphro is to appear as
prosecutor of his own father. Euthyphro's father had tied
up a peasant who killed another peasant in a drunken brawl,
notified the authorities, thrown the prisoner into a ditch,
and put the matter out of his mind; meanwhile the prisoner
died of hunger and cold. Euthyphro (Mr. Right-mind, as
Bunyan might have called him) feared lest the gods might
punish him if he sat at meat with a man who had done such
a deed, unless he set matters right by prosecuting the
offender. He must have known that this would be an
ineffectual gesture; the old-fashioned Homeric idea that
Zeus will punish men for callous insolence to the poor was
not going to impress the Athenian court.

Socrates (that is, I presume, Plato) finds it outrageous
that a man prosecutes his own father over the death of a
no-good peasant (he reiterates this term *'thēs'* to rub it in
how little the man's death mattered) and he tries to dissuade
Euthyphro by tricky arguments, in a style much admired
and imitated by modern moral philosophers. Euthyphro is
easily tied in knots by asking him whether pious deeds are
pious because they please the gods, or please the gods
because they are pious deeds; whether men ever disagree
except about moral matters, for which there is no decision
procedure like arithmetical calculation or physical measure-
ments; and so on. But Mr. Right-mind is not convinced;
again and again he cuts himself loose from these dialectical
knots with the assertion that it doesn't matter who was the
murderer and what relation he was to the prosecutor and
whether the victim was a peasant, but only whether a man
was foully done to death in a way that all the gods must
hate. The dialogue ends with Euthyphro telling Socrates he
has no more time for discussion and going off on his legal
business.

Was this, as the received view represents, a victory for
Socrates? Or was it a victory for simple piety over sophistical
tricks? Euthyphro admittedly had one weak point: he
believed in many gods who were sometimes at variance

with one another and so might command different things. But this is irrelevant for our purposes; for Euthyphro's unswerving fidelity to the divine law would be no less objectionable to modern moral philosophers if he had believed in one God. The main issue is whether a man's moral code ought to be influenced in this way by beliefs about Divine commands.

In the first place, I want to reject a view—which some Christians have at least approached—that all our appraisals of good and bad logically depend on knowledge of God. To get a clear and indisputable example I shall take a bad sort of act. For there is a logical asymmetry between good and bad acts: an act is good only if everything about it is good, but may be bad if *anything* about it is bad; so it might be risky to say we knew an act to be good *sans phrase*, rather than to have some good features. But there is no such risk in saying that we know certain kinds of act to be bad. Lying, for example, is bad, and we all know this; giving a man the lie is a deadly insult the world over.

If a philosopher says he doubts whether there is anything objectionable in the practice of lying, he is not to be heard. Perhaps he is not sincere in what he says; perhaps his understanding is debauched by wickedness; perhaps, as often happens to philosophers, he has been deluded by a fallacious argument into denying what he really knows to be the case. Anyhow, it does not lie in his mouth to say that here I am abandoning argument for abuse; there is something logically incongruous, to use Newman's phrase, if we take the word of a Professor of Lying that he does not lie. Let me emphasize that I am not saying a sane and honest man must think one should *never* lie; but I say that, even if he thinks lying is sometimes a necessary evil, a sane and honest man must think it an evil.

Now it is logically impossible that our knowledge that lying is bad should depend on revelation. For obviously a revelation from a deity whose 'goodness' did not include any objection to lying would be worthless; and indeed, so far from getting our knowledge that lying is bad from revelation, we may use this knowledge to test alleged revelations. Xenophanes rejected traditional Greek religious beliefs because the gods were represented as liars and cheats; and (if Browning could be trusted) it would be a fatal objection to the claims of the Druses' Messiah Hakim that he commanded his followers to lie about their religion under persecution. It is not that it would be too dreadful to believe in mendacious deities; a revelation destroys its own credibility if it is admitted to come from deities or from a prophet who may lie. We know lying to be bad before needing to examine any alleged revelation. Sir Arnold Lunn has jeered at unbelievers for esteeming truthfulness apart from any supernatural hopes or fears, and has quoted with approval a remark of Belloc that one can't be loyal to an abstraction like truth; a pagan Greek would have retorted that Lunn and Belloc were *akolastoi*, incorrigibly wicked, if they could not see directly the badness of lying.

The knowledge of God is thus *not* prerequisite to our having *any* moral knowledge. I shall argue however that we do need it in order to see that we must not do evil that good may come, and that this principle actually follows from a certain conception of God. If I can make this out, the sophistry from which I started will have been completely refuted; for accepting or rejecting this principle makes an enormous difference to one's moral code.

I must first clear up an ambiguity in the phrase 'doing evil that good may come'. We cannot ask whether e.g. Caesar's death was a good or bad *thing to happen;* there are *various* titles under which it may be called good or bad. One might very well say e.g. that a violent death was a bad *thing to happen to a living organism* but a good *thing to happen to a man who claimed divine worship*, and this would again leave it open whether doing Caesar to death was a good or bad *thing to do* for Brutus and the rest. Now when I speak of 'not doing evil that good may come', what I mean is that certain sorts of act are such *bad things to do* that they must never be done to secure any good or avoid any evil. For A to kill a man or cut off his arm is not necessarily a *bad thing to do*, though it is necessarily bad that such a thing should happen to a living organism. Only by a fallacy of equivocation can people argue that if you accept the principle of not doing evil that good may come, then you must be against capital punishment and surgical operations.

Suppose that A and B are agreed that adultery is a bad sort of behaviour, but that A accepts the principle of not doing evil that good may come, whereas B rejects it. Then in A's moral deliberations adultery is simply out: as Aristotle said, there can be no deliberating when and how and with whom to commit it (EN 1107a16). For B, on the other hand, the *prima facie* objection to adultery is defeasible, and in some circumstances he may decide: Here and now adultery is the best thing. Similarly, Sir David Ross holds that the objection to punishing the innocent, viz. that then we are not 'respecting the rights of those who have respected the rights of others', is only a *prima facie* objection; in the general interest it may have to be overruled, 'that the whole nation perish not'—a Scripture quotation that we may hope Sir David made without remembering who was speciously justifying whose judicial murder.

It is psychologically possible to hold the principle of not doing evil that good may come independently of any belief in Divine commandments: I have already cited the example of Aristotle on adultery. We have to see whether this is also logically consistent.

We must first settle what sort of answer is relevant if a man asks 'Why shouldn't I commit adultery?'; only then can we see what reason against, if any, is decisive. One obviously relevant sort of reply to a question 'Why shouldn't I?' is an appeal to something the questioner wants, and cannot get if he does so-and-so. I maintain that only such a reply is relevant and rational. In post-Kantian moral theory another sort of reply has been offered as relevant—an appeal not to an agent's Inclinations but to his Sense of Duty. Now indeed you can so train a man that 'You *must* not', said in a peculiar manner, strikes him as a sufficient answer to 'Why shouldn't I?'; he may feel a peculiar awe at hearing this from others, or even on saying it himself; it may even be part of the training to make him think he *must* not ask why he *must* not. (Cf. Lewis Carroll's juvenile poem 'My Fairy'.) The result of such training is what people like Sir David Ross call 'apprehending obligation'. When I speak of the Sense of Duty (in capitals) I shall always be referring to this notion.

Now, as we know, a totalitarian regime can make a man 'apprehend' all sorts of things as his 'obligations', if Providence does not specially protect him. But on the Sense of Duty theory a man so trained is admirable if he does what he thinks he *must* do, regardless of the nature and quality of his acts; for is he not acting from the highest of motives, the Sense of Duty? If a young Nazi machine-guns a column of refugees till he bleeds to death, instead of retiring for medical treatment, is not his Sense of Duty something to fill us with awe?

To myself, it seems clear that although '*You mustn't*' said in this peculiar way may psychologically work as a final answer to 'Why shouldn't I?', it is no rational answer at all. This Sense of Duty, as Bradley said (*Appearance and Reality*, c. 25) 'is empty self-will and self-assurance, which swollen with private sentiment or chance desire, wears the mask of goodness. And hence that which professes itself moral would be the same as mere badness, if it did not differ, even for the worse, by the addition of hypocrisy. We may note here that our country, the chosen home of Moral Philosophy, has the reputation abroad of being the chief home of hypocrisy and cant.'

Let us forget about the Sense of Duty, for I think it can be shown that an action's being a good or bad thing for a human being to do is of itself a fact calculated to touch an agent's inclinations. I shall here appropriate the powerful arguments, in the spirit of Aristotle, recently developed by Mrs. Philippa Foot. Moral virtues, she argues, are habits of action and avoidance; and they are such as a man cannot rationally choose to go without, any more than he can rationally choose to be blind, paralytic, or stupid; to choose to lack a virtue would be to choose a maimed life, ill-adapted to this difficult and dangerous world. But if you opt for virtue, you opt for being the sort of man who *needs* to act virtuously (just as if you choose to take up smoking you opt to be the kind of man who *needs* to smoke); moreover, you cannot decide at the outset to act virtuously only when it is not too awkward or dangerous or unpleasant—that is deciding not to have the habit of virtue at all. If, for example, you opt for courage, you may perish through facing danger a coward would have shirked; but our world is such that it is not even safe not to be brave—as Horace said, death pursues after cowards too. And if you opt for chastity, then you opt to become the sort of person who *needs* to be chaste; and then for you, as Aristotle said, there can be no deliberating when and with whom to commit adultery; adultery is out.

But somebody might very well admit that not only is there something bad about certain acts, but also it is desirable to become the sort of person who needs to act in the contrary way; and yet *not* admit that such acts are to be avoided in all circumstances and at any price. To be sure, a virtuous person cannot be ready in advance to do such acts; and if he does do them they will damage his virtuous habits and perhaps irreparably wreck his hard-won integrity of soul. But at this point someone may protest 'Are you the only person to be considered? Suppose the price of your precious integrity is a most fearful disaster! Haven't you got a hand to burn for your country (or mankind) and your friends?'. This sort of appeal has not, I think, been adequately answered on Aristotelian lines, either by Aristotle or by Mrs. Foot.

It is just at this point, I think, that the law of God becomes relevant. I shall not argue as to the truth of the theological propositions I shall use in the following discussion; my aim in this essay is to show that *if* a man accepts them he may rationally have quite a different code from someone who does not. And the propositions I shall use all belong to natural theology; in Hobbes's language, I am considering only 'the Kingdom of God by Nature'.

If God and Man are voluntary agents, it is reasonable to believe that God will not only direct men to his own ends willy-nilly like the irrational creatures, but will govern them by command and counsel. The question is then whether God has given laws to man which forbid whole classes of actions, as human laws do. There appear strong reasons for doubting whether God's commands could be like this.

> Laws have to be framed in broad general terms because the foresight of legislation is limited, and because the laws would be unmanageably complicated if the legislators even tried to bring in all the contingencies they could themselves foresee; nor can there be somebody always at every man's elbow to give him commands suiting the particular contingency. But God is subject to none of these human limitations; so it is not a grossly anthropomorphic view of God to imagine him legislating in general terms because hard cases make bad law?

It is not a question, I reply, of God's knowledge and power, but of man's. Man's reason can readily discern that certain practices, like lying, infanticide, and adultery, are generally undesirable, even to the point that it is generally desirable that men should not *think* of resorting to them. But what man is competent judge in his own cause, to make exception in a particular case? Even apart from bias, our knowledge of the present relevant circumstances is grossly fallible; still more, our foresight of the future. Some men, like Dr. Buchman's disciples, have claimed to have Divine guidance in all conjunctures of life; but such claims are open to doubt, and certainly most men are not thus favoured. So unless the rational knowledge that these practices are *generally undesirable* is itself a promulgation of the Divine law *absolutely forbidding* such practices, God has left most men without any promulgation of commands to them on these matters at all: which, on the theological premises I am assuming, is absurd.

The rational recognition that a practice is generally undesirable and that it is best for people on the whole not even to think of resorting to it is thus *in fact* a promulgation to a man of the Divine law forbidding the practice, even if he does not realise that this is a promulgation of the Divine law, even if he does not believe there is a God.

This is not a paradox. You have had a city's parking regulation promulgated to you by a No Parking notice, even if you are under the illusion that you may ignore the notice and think it has been put up by a neighbour who dislikes cars. And similarly anyone who can see the general objectionableness of lying and adultery has had God's law against such actions promulgated to him, even if he does not recognize it as God's law.

This means that the Divine law is in some instances promulgated to all men of sound understanding. No man can sincerely plead ignorance that lying, for example, is generally objectionable. I am *not* saying that a sane and honest man must see that lying is *absolutely excluded;* but he must have some knowledge of the *general objectionableness* of lying, and this is in fact a promulgation to him of the Divine law against lying. And he can advance from this knowledge to recognition of the Divine law as such, by a purely rational process.

To make this point clearer, let us consider a modern ethical philosopher who says 'I do on the whole object to lying, but this is just a practical attitude I take up—it is quite wrong to call it "knowledge" '. I do *not* say of him what I should of a man who professed to have no special objection to lying: that he is just a vicious fellow, or a fool talking at random, who deserves no answer. What I do say is that his very protest shows that he does possess that sort of knowledge which is in fact God's promulgation of a law to him. His erroneous philosophy will not allow him to call it knowledge; but that does not prevent it from *being* knowledge—philosophers in fact know many things that their own theories would preclude them from knowing. And since he has this knowledge, he has had God's law against lying promulgated to him, even if he does not believe in God.

Thus, whatever a man may think, his rational knowledge that it is a bad way of life for a man to be a liar or an adulterer is in fact a promulgation to him of the Divine law; and he is able to infer that it is such a promulgation if he rightly considers the matter. As Hobbes said:

> These dictates of reason men use to call by the name of laws, but improperly: for they are but conclusions or theorems concerning what conduceth to the conservation and defence of themselves: whereas law, properly, is the word of him that by right hath command over others. But yet if we consider the same theorems as delivered in the word of God that by right commandeth over all things, then are they properly called laws.

There is a current malicious interpretation of Hobbes on which 'the word of God' would mean whatever the sovereign chooses to decree to be canonical Scripture. High-minded people are prepared to talk about Hobbes with reckless disregard of the truth: the late Lord Lindsay, in his Preface to the Everyman *Leviathan*, perpetrated a serious garbling of Hobbes' text, giving the false text an air of authenticity by the use of antique spelling.[1] But what Hobbes himself says elsewhere is: 'God declareth his word by the dictates of natural reason.' As an historical footnote I add that a very similar line of reasoning is to be found in Berkeley's youthful sermon on Passive Obedience. The debt Berkeley owes to Hobbes is quite obvious: but no doubt a clergyman could hardly cite such an authority explicitly without destroying the edifying effect of his discourse.

But what if somebody asks 'Why should I obey God's Law?' This is really an insane question. For Prometheus to defy Zeus made sense because Zeus had not made Prometheus and had only limited power over him. A defiance of an Almighty God is insane: it is like trying to cheat a man to whom your whole business is mortgaged and who you know is well aware of your attempts to cheat him, or again, as the prophet said, it is as if a stick tried to beat, or an axe to cut, the very hand that was wielding it. Nebuchadnezzar had it forced on his attention that only by God's favour did his

---

[1] p. xvi of Everyman edition. Lindsay's garbling confounds Law and Right of Nature; which Hobbes emphatically distinguishes in the very passage (c. 14 *ad init.*) that Lindsay claims to be quoting!

wits hold together from one end of a blasphemous sentence to another—and so he saw that there was nothing for him but to bless and glorify the King of Heaven, who is able to abase those who walk in pride. To quote Hobbes again 'God is King, though the nations be angry: and he that sitteth upon the cherubim, though the earth be moved. Whether men will or no they must be subject always to the divine power. By denying the existence or providence of God, men may shake off their ease, but not their yoke.'

This reasoning will not convince everybody; people may still *say* that it makes sense, given that there is a God, to defy him; but this is so only because, as Prichard said, you can no more make a man think than you can make a horse drink. A moral philosopher once said to me: 'I don't think I am morally obliged to obey God unless God is good: and surely it is a synthetic proposition that God is good.' I naturally asked him how he understood the proposition that God is good; he replied 'Well, I have no considered view how it should be analysed; but provisionally I'd say it meant something like this: God is the sort of God whom I'd choose to be God if it were up to me to make the choice.' I fear he has never understood why I found the answer funny.

I shall be told by such philosophers that since I am saying not: It is your supreme moral duty to obey God, but simply: It is insane to set about defying an Almighty God, my attitude is plain power-worship. So it is: but it is worship of the Supreme power, and as such is wholly different from, and does not carry with it, a cringing attitude towards earthly powers. An earthly potentate does not compete with God, even unsuccessfully: he may threaten all manner of afflictions, but only from God's hands can any affliction actually come upon us. If we fully realize this, we shall have such fear of God as destroys all earthly fear: 'I will show you whom you shall fear', said Jesus Christ to his disciples.

'But now you are letting your view of the facts distort your values.' I am not sure whether this piece of claptrap is meant as moral reprobation or as a logical objection; either way, there is nothing in it. Civilized men know that sexual intercourse is liable to result in child-bearing; they naturally have quite different sexual morals, one way or another, from savages who do not know this. And they are logically justified in evaluating sexual intercourse differently; for they have a different view of what sort of act it is. Now for those who believe in Almighty God, a man's every act is an act either of obeying or of ignoring or of defying that God; so naturally and logically they have quite different standards from unbelievers—they take a different view as to what people are in fact doing.

'But suppose circumstances are such that observance of one Divine law, say the law against lying, involves breach of some other absolute Divine prohibition?'—If God is rational, he does not command the impossible; if God governs all events by his providence, he can see to it that circumstances in which a man is inculpably faced by a choice between forbidden acts do not occur. Of course such circumstances (with the clause 'and there is no way out' written into their description) are consistently describable; but God's providence could ensure that they do not in fact arise. Contrary to what unbelievers often say, belief in the existence of God does make a difference to what one expects to happen.

Let us then return to our friend Euthyphro. Euthyphro regarded his father's act of leaving a poor man to die forgotten in a ditch as not just *prima facie* objectionable, but as something *forbidden* by the gods who live for ever; and he was horribly afraid for himself if he went on living with the offender as if nothing had happened. He did well to be afraid, the fear of God is the beginning of wisdom. To be sure, it is not all of wisdom.

The fear of God of which I have spoken is such fear as restrains even the wish to disobey him; not merely servile fear, which restrains the outward act, but leaves behind the wish 'If only I could do it and get away with it!' And, as is proper in a paper of this kind, I have confined myself to what Hobbes called the Kingdom of God by Nature. It is no part of our merely natural knowledge of God that we can boldly call God our Father and serve him in filial love: we are his children, if we are, purely by his free gift of the Spirit of adoption, and not by birthright: and the fear of God for his power irresistible is at least the *beginning* of wisdom—without it there is only pitiable folly. I agree, indeed, with Hobbes that gratitude for God's benefits would not be a sufficient ground for *unreserved* obedience if it were severed from fear of God's irresistible power.

That fear is an ultimate suasion. We cannot balance against our obedience to God some good to be gained, or evil to be avoided, by disobedience. For such good or evil could in fact come to us only in the order of God's Providence; we cannot secure good or avoid evil, either for ourselves or for others, in God's despite and by disobedience. And neither reason nor revelation warrants the idea that God is at all likely to be lenient with those who presumptuously disobey his law because of the way they have worked out the respective consequence of obedience and disobedience. Eleazer the scribe (2 Maccabees 6), with only Sheol to look forward to when he died, chose rather to go there by martyrdom—*praemitti se velle in infernum*—than to break God's law. 'Yet should I not escape the hand of the Almighty, neither alive nor dead.'

The wicked can for the moment use God's creation in defiance of God's commandments. But this is a sort of miracle or mystery; as St. Paul said, God has made the creature subject to vanity against its will. It is reasonable to expect, if the world's whole *raison d'être* is to effect God's good pleasure, that the very natural agents and operations of the world should be such as to frustrate and enrage and torment those who set their wills against God's. If things are not at present like this, that is only a gratuitous mercy, on whose continuance the sinner has no reason to count. 'The world shall fight with him against the unwise. . . . Yea, a mighty wind shall stand up against them, and like a storm shall blow them away.'

Index

abstract noun, 46 f., 50 f.
 noun-phrase, 42, 47–52, 69 f., 81 f.
accidental individuals, 68–70
activity:
 basic, 32 ff.
 characteristic, 73
 of thinking, 30–7
acts, mental:
 of judgment, 12
 meaning conferred by?, 20 f., 31 f.
 of thought, 22, 30–7, 72
 of understanding, 31
 of will, 22
actuality:
 change and, 65 f., 72
 changeless, eternal, 73 f.
 existence and, 58 ff., 65 f.
 Frege on, 65 f.
 imperfect, 72
 time needed for, 72 f.
actus essendi, see esse
adultery, 121 f., 123 f., 126
agents, *see* rational agents
Ambler, E., 74
analogical language, 55, 76, 81
Anaxagoras, 104, 105 f., 114
angels, 64, 77
anger, 19, 22, 90
animals, minds of, 2, 19
animation, 1, 3
Anscombe, G. E. M., 32 f.
Anselm, St., 57
anti-materialists, 30
Apocalypse, the, 100
Aquinas, St. Thomas:
 on 'acts of understanding', 31
 on angels, 64, 77

Aquinas, St. Thomas—*continued*
 on changelessness of God., 93, 98
 on creation, 83 f.
 on 'Dionysius', 50
 on *ens* and *entis*, 58
 on *esse*, 42, 57, 59–64
  naturale) (*intentionale*, 63 f.
 on *est*, 42, 57, 60
 his five ways, 77
 on forms, 42 f., 45 f., 48 f.
  individualized, 51, 60–4
  Platonic, 46
  subsistent, 46, 51, 64
 on God's simplicity, 52
 multiplicity relates to forms, 45
 on necessary beings, 77
 on predication, 43 f.
 on *quo*, 42
 on relationships, 69
 on the soul, 23, 28, 77
  disembodied, 22, 28
  'my—is not I', 22, 40
 on 'spiritual matter', 23 f.
Aristotle:
 on adultery, 121, 123
 astronomy in, 94
 on change, 72
 on Empedocles, 92
 physics in, 94
 'the praise is vulgar', 105
 on the soul, 38
 on syllogism, 79
 on thinking, 31
 on virtues, 122 f.
arithmetic, 66 ff.
 see also numbers
ascription of actions, 4, 33 f.

ascriptivism, 4
astral worship, *see* worship
astronomy, 56, 94 f.
attributes, 51, 68
Augustine, St., of Canterbury, 109
of Hippo, 110
Augustus, 59
Austin, J. L., 12 f.
Ayer, A. J., 12 f.

bad(ness), *see* evil
baptized reason, 75
basic activities, 32 ff.
'because', 82, 87 f.
Begriffe (concepts):
and forms, 45 f., 49, 52, 60
functional nature of, 49 f.
marks or notes (*Merkmale*) of, 46
multiplicity applies to, 46
properties (*Eigenschaften*) of, 46
Begriffswort, 56, 60
behaviourism, 21
Belloc, H., 120
Berkeley, G., 126
body, human:
continuity of, 26–8
fusion or fission of, 26
see also subtle body
body-mind relation, 1, 17
see also animation, soul
bona fides not enough, 5, 15, 20, 27, 31,
100, 111
Boolean functions, 80
Bradley, F. H.:
on moral philosophy, 122
on spiritualism, 26
on time, 93
brain, 30, 37
brain-processes, 19, 37, 71
brainwashing, 14 f., 89, 104, 122
Bridey Murphy, 2, 16
Bridges, R., 89
Browning, R., 120
Buchman, F., 124
Buddhists, 2

Caesar, *see* Julius Caesar
'Cambridge' changes, 71 f., 99
Cambridge Platonists, 117
Carroll, Lewis:
croquet in, 97
his diagrams, 80
on Nobody, 44
on predication, 43
'You mustn't', 122

causal:
arguments, 75
hypotheticals, 82
propositions, 75–8, 81–5, 88
causality, principle of, 96
chance, *see* contingency, probability
change, 65 f.:
is in creatures, not God, 93, 98 f.
criticism of 71, f., 99
genuine vs. 'Cambridge', 66, 72, 99
character, persistence of, 5, 24
characteristic activities, 73
charity, 115 f.
choice, free, 22, 87, 97
Christ:
his coming, 29, 86
his death, 93, 107, 121
on fear of God, 127
on persecution, 115
on prayer, 86 f.
relics of?, 107
resurrection of, 107
Christian belief:
apologetic for, 92 f., 96 f.
in Christ's death, 93
about the Eucharist, 107 f.
in impetration, 87
in the Incarnation, 107
in prayer, 86
in the resurrection of the body, 29, 40
Christian Science, 86, 92
clockability:
of mental images, 36
of murders, 37
of non-basic activities, 37
of sensory processes, 36
of thoughts, 36
cogito, 6 f., 10
concepts, psychological, 19–22
see also Begriffe
concussion, effects of, 4, 14
conditionals, unfulfilled, 32, 88 f.
consistency proofs, 67, 107
contingency, 77, 90, 93–7
continuity:
bodily, 26–8
of memory, 14 f., 27 f.
mental, 27 f.
physical (real), 22
of thoughts?, 34 f.
conventionalist sulk, 3, 11
Cook Wilson, J., 12
corpses, 28, 107
creation, 83 f.

creatures, are changeable and temporal, 92 f.
criteria, *see* inner criteria *and* identity
croquet, when playable, 97
Cutler, Sir J., 27

damned, the, 22, 129
De Ente et Essentia, 46
death, *see* soul, survival, resurrection
decision procedure, 67, 79, 118
deduction, 78–81
degenerate (equations, uses of words), 8
demythologizing, 67 f.
Descartes, R.:
  his *cogito*, 6 f., 10
  'I' means something immaterial, 7 f., 38
  masked man fallacy in, 8
  mind = person for him, 2
  'who' question in, 7, 9
descriptions, definite, 58, 110 f.
'determined in causes', events, 94, 96
determinism, 96 f.
dictionary ignored, 11
differentiation, 23 f., 26
  see also souls
disembodied minds, souls, spirits:
  see remnant, mind, soul, spirit
dollatry, 103
Doyle, Sir A. C., 113
Druses, 120
dulia, 101 f.
Duty, Sense of, 121 f.

Eigenschaft, 46
ego, 7
electrons, 18
Empedocles, 92
'*es gibt*', 8 f., 65
esse, est, see Aquinas, St. Thomas
eternity, 73 f., 88, 93, 99
Eucharist, 107 f.
Euthyphro, 117 ff., 128
events, *see* occurrences
evil:
  existence of, 57
  kinds of act, 119
  'that good may come', 120 f.
existence, existential propositions:
  denial of, 54–6, 58
  '*es gibt*' sense of, 56, 65
  see also actuality, *esse*, 'there is', 'God exists'
experiences:
  identity of, 19 f.

experiences—*continued*
  memory-, 13
  private, 18 ff.
  see also acts, mental *and* activities
extrapolation, 81
Ezechias, king of Juda, 97 f.

facts, 68 ff.
fait accompli, 90, 93, 99
faith, *see* Christian belief
Farrer, A., 97
Fatherhood of God, 102, 129
fear, 22, 89
  of God, 127 ff.
feelings, 21 f., 34 f.
Fermat, P., 95 n.
fission, 26
Flew, A. G. N., 3
Foot, P., 122 f.
forgiveness of sins, 101 f., 111
forms:
  abstract nouns and, 46 ff.
  and functions, 49 f., 52
  multiplicity applies to, 45
  Plato on, 46, 48, 50 f.
  predicativeness of, 43
  see also Aquinas, St. Thomas; individualized forms; *Begriffe*
Frege, G.:
  on *Begriffe*, 45–8, 56
  on *Eigenschaft* amd *Merkmal*, 65
  on '*es gibt*', 65
  on functions, 49, 52
  on levels of concepts, 65
  on *Wirklichkeit*, 65
Freud, S., 4, 8
functions, *see* forms; *Begriffe*; Frege, G.
fusion, 24, 26

Gentiles, 100
  see also heathen ways
geometry, 66–8, 72 f.
glory, 86, 102
God:
  above logic?, 85, 105
  actual, 74
  cause of changeable things, 81, 92 f., 105
  commandments of, 117; *see* law, Divine
  Creator, *see* creation, creature
  esse of, 60 f.
  eternity of, 73 f., 88, 93, 99
  see also change

God—*continuea*
  goodness of, 127
  'I am', said by, 58
  is incorporeal, 105 f.
  as Judge, 4, 111, 129
  as King, 74, 124, 126–9
  needs creatures?, 114
  omniscience of, 90, 93
  is Power irresistible, 51, 126 ff.
  his presence in creatures, 106 ff.
  as rational agent, 87, 96, 124
  simplicity of, 52
  superannuated?, 58 f.
  has timeless view of the world?, 90, 92 f.
  timelessness of ?, 74
  is unchanging, 73 f., 80, 93, 98 f., 105 f.
  is Wisdom itself, 51
  see also Providence; law, Divine
'God', the term:
  descriptive force of, 57 f., 109
  not a proper name, 57, 108 f.
'God exists':
  logical status of, 57, 114 f.
  proof of, 75 ff., 80 f., 83, 85
Gods, English, 109
Gods, Greek, 58, 104, 118 f., 128
Gods, Hindu, 87, 104
Goedel, K., 67
Goering, H., reincarnation of, 25
goodness:
  of God, 127
  of occurrences, 119 f.
grace, God's, 86, 89 f., 102, 111, 129
Greek religion, 58, 104, 118 ff., 126, 128

hallucinations, 5, 18
hearing, 19, 22
heathen ways:
  astral worship, 104
  idolatry, 103 f.
  oracles, 105
  polytheism, 102, 118 f.
Heaven, 86
Hebrew grammar, 48
hell, 89; *see also* damned, the
Hindus, 2, 87, 104
Hitler, A., reincarnation of, 24 f.
Hobbes, T.:
  on God's Law, 126
  on God's Power, 127 ff.
  on the Kingdom of God by Nature, 124, 126 ff.

Hobbes, T.—*continued*
  slanders against, 117, 126
  on vain philosophy, 69
holes, 70
Holmes, S., 113
Homer, 58
Hopkins, G. M., 89 f., 102 f.
human beings:
  are animals, 38
  birth of, 6, 10
  bodies of, 2 f., 26–8, 38
  God's image in, 106
  'I' referring to, 6 ff.
  identity of, 6, 22 ff., 67
  proper names of, 6 f.
  survival of, 22
Hume, D.:
  on causal propositions, 75 f.
  on judging and breathing, 12
  on a superannuated God, 59 f.
Humphrey, G., 35
hypnosis, 13 f., 89
hysteria, 21 f., 25

'I':
  Descartes on, 6 ff.
  McTaggart on, 6 t.
  propositions containing, 5–10, 27
  reference of:
    immaterial?, 7 f.
    to a personality, 9 f.
    to the same man, 6
  soliloquistic use of, 6–10
identity, criteria of:
  for attributes, 51, 68
  for events, 71, 82
  for experiences, 20
  for human beings, 6, 26 ff., 67
    see also personal identity
  for lacks of care, 82
  for meanings, 68
  for numbers, 67
  for personalities, 9 f.
  for persons, *see* personal identity
  for relationships, 69
  for souls, 23–6
idolatry, 103–6, 116
  of machines, 41, 104 f.
ignorance of God, 111–13, 126
images (mental, visual), 20, 22, 34, 36
immaterialism, 30, 38
immateriality (of minds, selves, souls), 7 f., 18, 30
imperatives, 90 f.
impetration, 87 ff.

Index

Incarnation, 106 f.
inclinations, 121 f.
individualized forms, 50–3, 69 f.
individuals, 43, 46, 58, 65, 82
inner criteria, 11 f., 13, 20
inspiration, Divine, 112, 124
instruments, 33 f.
intensity, 61 f.
intentionality, 63 f., 84, 108 ff.
Isaias, 97
Izzard-Wye, J., 110 ff.

James, W., 34 f.
Johnson, S., 108
Judaism, 29, 74, 85, 93, 100, 103, 129
judgment, 12
Judgment Day, 4
Julius Caesar, reincarnation of, 2, 4, 10 f., 15

Kant, I., 36, 79
Keble, Warden of, 97
Kehama, The Curse of, 87
knowledge, 11 ff.
    'only he can have known', 15, 24 f.

language, structure of, 39
larvatus fallacy, 8
latria, 101 f., 108
law, Divine, 102, 123 f.
    consistency of, 128
    and human law, 124
    promulgation of, 124 ff.
Laws, Plato's, 104
Lewis, C. S., 90 ff., 96
Lindsay, Lord, 126
Locke, J., 3 f., 30
logic, 35, 77, 82
    God not above—, 85, 105
love, 5; for God, 111, 129
Lunn, Sir A., 120
lying, 119 f., 124 f., 128

Maccabeus, Judas, 29
Macdonald, J. R., 109
machines, 40 f., 104 f.
Macmillan, H., 109 f., 114
McTaggart, J. McT. E.:
    on change, 71
    on creation, 93
    on indubitable empirical truths, 7
    on love, 5
    'mind = person', 2
    on selves (and their parts), 6 f., 72

McTaggart, J. McT. E.—*continued*
    on time, 93
magnetic sensations, 21 f.
Malcolm, N., 36
man, men, *see* human beings
martyrdom, 29, 129
Mary, the Blessed Virgin, 101 f.
masked man fallacy, 8
materialism, 30, 37
mathematics, 8, 65, 77, 79
    see also arithmetic, geometry, numbers
matter:
    continuity in, 26 ff.
    differentiation of, 23 f., 26
    identity of, 26 ff.
    man is made with—, 7
    'spiritual', 23 f.
meaning, 19 ff., 31 f., 68
medieval philosophers, 23 f., 31, 77, 94
medium, immaterial, 24
    spirit—, 15, 25
memory:
    effacement of, 4, 14
    is episodic, 12 f.
    hypnotically produced, 13 f.
    and identity, 3, 4, 14 f., 28
    photographs and, 14
    of pre-existence, 3, 10 f., 24 f., 27 f.
    provenance of, 13 ff., 28
    responsibility and, 13
    unreliability of, 11 f.
memory-belief, -knowledge, 11
mental acts, *see* acts, mental
Mental Acts, 12
Méré, Chevalier de, 95
Merkmal, 46
'messages' from disembodied spirits, 15, 25 f., 39
Messiah, *see* Christ:
    of the Druses, 120
metamorphosis, 1 f.
metaphysical vision, 77
metempsychosis, 1 f.
mind:
    disembodied, 22 f.
    = person?, 2 f.
    plurality of -s, 22 f.
    = soul, 18
    survival of, 14 f., 22, 27 f., 39 f.
miracles, 86 f., 94, 97, 104
missionaries, 109, 115
modus ponens, 13
Moore, G. E., 11

moral:
  attitudes, 4, 125
  codes, 119 f., 124, 127 f.
  knowledge, 119 f., 122, 124 f.
  philosophers, 117 ff., 121 f., 125, 127
  responsibility, 4, 103, 111
multiplicity:
  applies to *Begriffe*, 46
  to forms, 44 f.
'*must*', 121 f.
mysterious entities, 66 f., 82

names, *see* proper names
natural theology, *see* theology
necessary beings, 77
needs, human, 123
neo-scholastic views, 31, 79, 98
Newman, Cardinal, 119 f.
Nielsen, H., 10
'nobody', 44, 67
nominalizations, 69 f., 82
'nothing', 67, 85
numbers, 67, 72, 74

objectionable, 121, 125, *see also* evil
objects, *see* individuals
obligations, 'apprehension' of, 122
occurrences, 70–2, 81 f.
Octavian, 59
oecumenism, 100
'of', senses of, 48 ff.
ontic commitment, 66
ontological arguments, 57, 59 f.
oracles, 105
Otto, R., 105
Oxford philosophers, 4

pain, 6 ff., 18–22, 36
Papists, 116
paraphrase, 47, 66, 69–71, 82
Parmenides, 92
Pascal, B., 95
Passmore, J., 6 f., 74 n.
past, prayers about the, 89 ff., 93 f.
past future tense, 88, 97 f.
Paul, St., 28, 100, 108, 129
paulo post futurum, 91
performatory analyses 12
persecution, 29, 104, 115, 120
personal identity:
  memory and, 3, 14 f., 27 f.
  and mind's identity, 2 f.
  moral attitudes and, 4
personality:
  identity of, 9 f.

personality—*continued*
  illusions of, 10
  multiple, 2, 9 f.
  transfer of, 10
Phaedo, 18
phenomenalism, 18
photographs and memory, 14
physicists, 18, 39, 96, 112 f.
pi, prayers about, 90 f.
Platonic dialogues:
  see Euthyphro, Laws, Phaedo, Sophist
  and *Theaetetus*
Platonic doctrines:
  on astral worship, 104, 106
  on existence, 66
  on Forms, 46, 48, 50 f
  on persecution, 104
  on the soul, 18 f., 38
polytheism, 102, 118 f.
Pope, A., 96
post-hypnotic suggestion, 13
Prague, 'Holy Infant' of, 104
prayer, 86–91, 93, 97
  for the dead, 29
  is *latria*, 102
  the Lord's, 86
  retrospective, 89–91, 93 f.
  to the Saints, 102
  see also impetration
predicates, predication:
  abstract nouns and, 49
  Aquinas on, 43 f.
  Lewis Carroll on, 43
  two-name theory of, 43 f.
prediction, 96
premises and conclusion, 75, 78 ff.
Prescott, W. H., 101
Priapists, 116
Prichard, H. A., 53
princesse lointaine, 108, 111
'principle, in', 71, 94 f., 96
probability, laws of, 95
proper name(s):
  of false Gods, 109
  of human beings, 7
  make-believe, 55 f.
  of personalities, 9
  'God' is not a —, 57 f., 109
  tenselessness of, 59
  translation, transliteration of, 109
Providence, Divine, 96 f., 122, 126 f.
pseudo-suppositions, 5, 14
psychical research, 15 25 f., 29
Pythagoreans, 71, 74

Index

quadratics, degenerate, 8
quantification, 66, 83 f.
questions, sense of, 7
Quine, W. V. O., 66, 80 f.
quo, 42

radiation, hard, 112 f.
rational agent(s), 87 f., 124
red-patch philosophy, 52 f.
reference, loss of, 8 f.
referring, 110 f.
reincarnation, 1 ff., 4 f., 10 f., 15 f., 24 f.
relational terms, 80 f.
relationships, 68 f.
remembering, *see* memory
remnant of a person, mental, 22 f., 39 f.
responsibility, moral, 4, 103
resurrection, 3, 28 f., 40, 107
reunion with body, soul's, 23, 28
revelation, 86, 119 f., 129
Roman Church, 101
Ross, Sir W. D., 121
Russell, B., 71, 110
Rutherford, 'Judge', 2
Ryle, G., 81

sacrifice, 101
Saints, 86, 101 f.
Schroeder, G., 68
Scriptural language, 38, 74, 100, 105 f.
seeing, 19–22
self, 6 f., 72, *see* person
senile: God, 59; voter, 109 ff., 114
sensation, sensory processes, 21 f., 36
sets, 68
sexual intercourse, 127 f.
Skinner, B. F., 34
Socrates' fallacy, 40
soliloquy, 6–9
Sophist, 66
souls, disembodied:
    fusion of, 24
    immortality of, 28
    number of, 22 f.
    reunion to body of, 23, 28
    sensory processes impossible in, 22, 40
    survival of, 22 f., 25, 28 f., 40
souls, embodied:
    Aristotle on, 38
    creation of, 83
    immaterial part of man?, 38
    Plato on, 18 f.
    are what we think with?, 18 f., 30, 38
souls, individuation of, 23
sounds, 62, 71

Southey, R., 87
Spinoza, B., 93, 96, 114
spirit, disembodied, 22 ff., 39 f.
spiritual matter, 23 f.
Strawson, P. F., 110
subtle bodies, 17 f.
sulks, conventionalist, 3, 11
superstition, subjects of:
    death, 38
    idols, *see* idolatry
    Infant of Prague, 104
    machines, 41, 104 f.
    numbers, 67, 74
    'relics' of Christ's body, 107
    scientific prediction, 96
    stars, 104, 106
    witches, 103
'support', intentionality of, 109 f.
suppositum, 43, 82
surfaces, 53, 70
surgeon, the mad, 14 f., 28 n.
survival of death, 3, 17, 22, 40
syllogistic, 79 f.
systematically misleading expression, 81

taking for granted, 12
Tarski, A., 67 f.
tenses, 88, 91, 97 f.
Theaetetus, 72, 99
theologians, theology:
    God of, 74, 113–15
    natural, 105, 113–15
    theses of, 74, 98, 105, 107, 115
'there is', 8 f., 57, 65, 67, 115
    see also 'God exists'
thinking, thought:
    activity of, 30
    actuality of, 63, 65, 72 f.
    is a basic activity, 34
    clockable?, 36 f.
    is discontinuous, 34 f.
    inner complexity of, 34 f.
    James on, 34 f.
    language and, 39
    long or short?, 36 ff.
    machines and, 40 f.
    organ(ism)s and, 38 ff.
thought, objects of:
    changed by thought?, 66, 72, 99
    esse of, 62 ff.
    reality of, 62 f., 110, 113 f.
Tichborne trial, 27
Tillich, P., 74
time:
    God and, 73 f., 91 ff.

time—*continued*
  Kantian (Newtonian) view of, 36
  machines, 5
  pictures of, 73 f.
  reality of, 91 ff.
Trinity, the Blessed, 102, 109
truth-drugs, 14, 27
two-name theory, 43 f.
Tyndall, J., 96

understanding, acts or feelings of, 5, 14, 31
universe of discourse, 80 f.

Venn diagrams, 80
verification, 78 f.
virtues, 122 f.
Voltaire, 95
Von Wright, G. H., 95
Vulcan, the planet, 56

waves, 53
weather, contingency of the, 95f.
Wells, H. G., 5, 72
Whitehead, A. N., 68
'who?' questions, 7, 9
'why not?', 121 f.
will, 22, 96 f.
  Divine, 86, 90, 97 f.
Wilson, H., 108 f.

Wilson, J. Cook, 12
Wirklichkeit, 65
witchcraft, 103
Wittgenstein, L.:
  on acts of mind, 32
  on decision procedures, 79
  on grammatical investigations, 32
  on identifying an experience, 20
  on mathematical proof, 79
  on meaning, 31 f.
  on names, 58 f.
  on pain, 19
  on sentence structure, 39
world, beginning of, 74
  see also creation, God
worship:
  associative, 101
  astral, 104, 106
  Gentile, 100
  intentionality of, 108
  natural theologian's, 114
  of a *nothing*, 108
  of Power, 127
  see also heathen ways, *dulia, latria*
    idolatry, dollatry, superstition

Xenophanes, 120
X-rays, 18

zero, 67